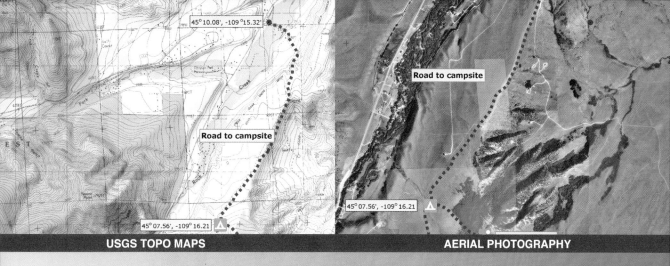

Stoeger Publishing
Great Outdoor Books Since 1925

STOEGER PUBLISHING COMPANY
IS A DIVISION OF BENELLI U.S.A.

BENELLI U.S.A.
Vice President and General Manager:
   Stephen Otway
Director of Brand Marketing and Communications:
   Stephen McKelvain

STOEGER PUBLISHING COMPANY
President: Jeffrey Reh
Publisher: Jay Langston
National Sales Manager: Cheryl Crowell
Managing Editor: Harris J. Andrews
Design & Production Director:
   Cynthia T. Richardson
Photography Director: Alex Bowers
Imaging Specialist: William Graves
Sales Manager Assistant: Julie Brownlee
Editorial Assistant: Christine Lawton
Administrative Assistant: Shannon McWilliams
Proofreader: Celia Beattie

Published by Stoeger Publishing Company
17603 Indian Head Highway, Suite 200
Accokeek, Maryland 20607

BK0310
ISBN: 0-88317-254-2

Library of Congress Control Number: 2002110079

Manufactured in the United States of America.

Distributed to the book trade and
to the sporting goods trade by:
Stoeger Industries
17603 Indian Head Highway, Suite 200
Accokeek, Maryland 20607
301-283-6300 Fax: 301-283-6986
www.stoegerindustries.com

OTHER PUBLICATIONS:

Shooter's Bible 2004 - 95th Edition
   The World's Standard Firearms
   Reference Book
Gun Trader's Guide - 26th Edition
   Complete Fully Illustrated
   Guide to Modern Firearms with
   Current Market Values

HUNTING & SHOOTING
Elk Hunter's Bible
Shotgunning for Deer
The Turkey Hunter's Tool Kit:
   Shooting Savvy
Hunting Whitetails East & West
Archer's Bible
The Truth About
   Spring Turkey Hunting
   According to "Cuz"
The Whole Truth About
   Spring Turkey Hunting
   According to "Cuz"
Complete Book of Whitetail Hunting
Hunting and Shooting
   with the Modern Bow
The Ultimate in Rifle Accuracy
Advanced Black Powder Hunting
Hounds of the World
Labrador Retrievers
Hunting America's Wild Turkey
Taxidermy Guide
Cowboy Action Shooting
Great Shooters of the World

COLLECTING BOOKS
Sporting Collectibles
The Working Folding Knife

FIREARMS
Antique Guns
P-38 Automatic Pistol
The Walther Handgun Story
Firearms Disassembly
   with Exploded Views
Rifle Guide
Gunsmithing at Home

Complete Guide to Modern Rifles
Complete Guide to Classic Rifles
Legendary Sporting Rifles
FN Browning Armorer to the World
Modern Beretta Firearms
How to Buy & Sell Used Guns
Heckler & Koch:
   Armorers of the Free World
Spanish Handguns

RELOADING
The Handloader's Manual of
   Cartridge Conversions
Modern Sporting Rifle Cartridges
Complete Reloading Guide

FISHING
Ultimate Bass Boats
Bassing Bible
The Flytier's Companion
Deceiving Trout
The Complete Book of Trout Fishing
The Complete Book of Flyfishing
Peter Dean's Guide to Fly-Tying
The Flytier's Manual
Handbook of Fly Tying
The Fly Fisherman's Entomological
   Pattern Book

MOTORCYCLES & TRUCKS
The Legend of Harley-Davidson
The Legend of the Indian
Best of Harley-Davidson
Classic Bikes
Great Trucks
4X4 Vehicles

COOKING GAME
Fish & Shellfish Care & Cookery
Game Cookbook
Dress 'Em Out
Wild About Venison
Wild About Game Birds
Wild About Freshwater Fish
Wild About Waterfowl
The Lore of Spices

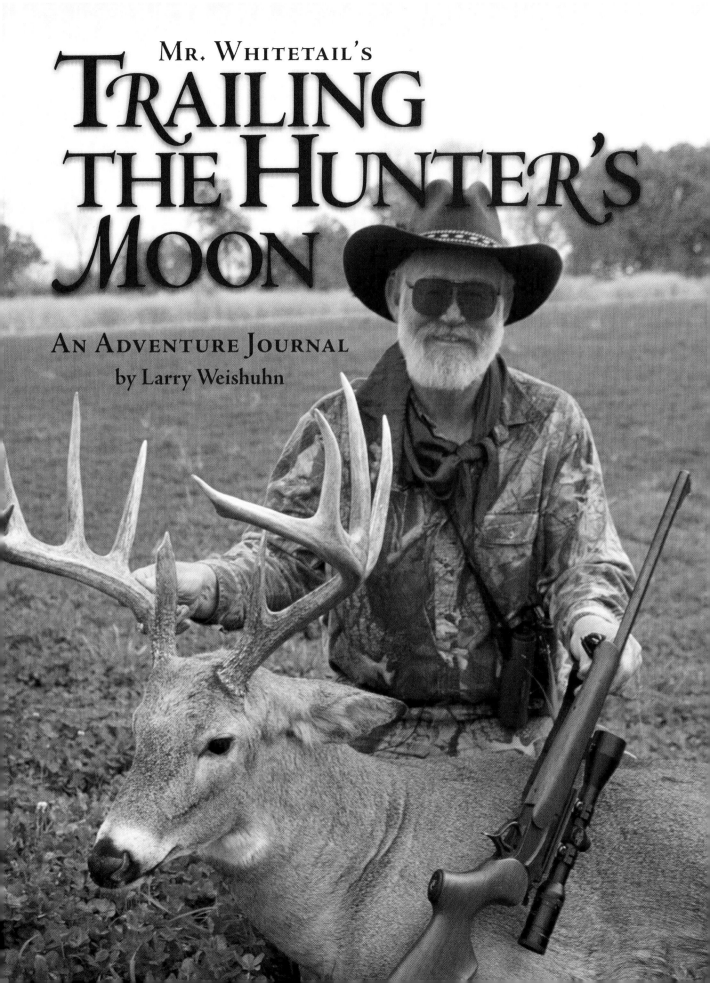

Mr. Whitetail's
Trailing the Hunter's Moon

An Adventure Journal
by Larry Weishuhn

DEDICATION

Trailing the Hunters Moon
is dedicated to the many friends, acquaintances,
guides and outfitters
with whom I've spent time in hunting camps,
especially those mentioned in this book,
as well as to the animals I've successfully
and unsuccessfully pursued.
Thanks to the hunt they live on and on.
Trailing the Hunters Moon
is foremost dedicated to my grandchildren;
Jake, Andrew and Katy Rose Johnson, and, Joshua and Justin Gonzalez
in hopes they too may someday experience
the great outdoor adventures their "Popo" has.
The pleasures and pride they have given me are priceless!
To my daughters Theresa and Beth,
and my wife, Mary Anne,
who didn't give up when others would have,
Thank You!

CONTENTS

ACKNOWLEDGMENTS

As a youngster growing up in rural Texas during the 1950s, hunting was sometimes an escape from hard work, but so was reading about the hunting adventures of Jack O'Connor, Elmer Keith, Byron Dalrymple, Russell Annabel, and others. When time permitted during the day and sometimes at night, for my dad was passionate about hunting with hounds, we hunted.

When I couldn't accompany my dad on hunts my mother would read to me from the pages of *Sports Afield, Outdoor Life* and occasionally *Field & Stream* and *Argosy,* long before I knew how to read. But, that also didn't stop me from looking at photographs and dreaming of someday hunting the animals pursued by my heroes. Later, when I did learn to read I spent whatever time possible paging through hunting and shooting journals, reading and dreaming.

I remember sitting next to my mother as she read to me and telling her that someday I'd hunt in Alaska, Canada, Africa and Europe. Little did I realize that someday those dreams would actually come true.

I have been extremely fortunate. As with hunting, timing is extremely important in life. I came along at a time when thanks to air travel I could be in nearly any hunting camp within a couple of days. And this was at a time when there was much game to hunt, thanks in part to proper game management, there being an economic value on wildlife which helped sustain wild populations, and at a time when our climates were conducive to producing excellent wildlife habitats. For this I am extremely thankful!

Many of the tales you'll read in this book have previously been written about in the pages of the numerous hunting and shooting journals for which I've written, either as a freelance or staff writer. In different forms they have appeared in such publications as *Shooting Times, North American Hunter, American Hunter, Petersen's Hunting, Handgunning, Rifle, Deer & Deer Hunting, Safari, Sporting Classics, Game Trails* and *The Texas Hunting Directory.* I am most grateful to the editors of these excellent publications in allowing me to write about those hunting tales again here in this book. Several of the hunts written about in this book were also filmed for television shows and appeared on such productions as "Realtree Outdoors," "Bass Pro's Outdoor World," and others, as well as my own show that aired on the Outdoor Channel, "Larry Weishuhn's Hunting the World."

I am also extremely grateful to Jay Langston and others at Stoeger Publishing for allowing me to do this book. It is one I have long wanted to write.

FOREWORD

It's about time. I've been looking forward to Larry Weishuhn's new book ever since I read the last one, and I wasn't disappointed with this work. I'm sure you won't be either.

I've known Larry for many years, and he's always been one of my favorite hunting buddies. As one who has been a full-time hunting writer for 25 years, I've met most of the folks in our business. Some are great writers and so-so hunters, sort of like Howard Cosell who was extremely knowledgeable about football and wrote the book, *"I Never Played the Game."* Unlike Cosell, Larry has played the game, and he's a great writer to boot.

I've been on a number of hunts with Larry and have plenty of memories. I remember a moose hunt in Colorado, where Larry and I had drawn precious nonresident lottery tags. He ended up getting a fine bull, which was par for the course. The week before, he took a great bull in Maine. No surprise there. Larry is usually successful on his hunts, but when he isn't, he's not afraid to admit it in print. I know plenty of writers whose egos prevent them from telling the truth. In this book, you'll read about some misses that he candidly reveals.

I recall another hunt in Texas when we chased nilgai with blackpowder rifles. It was no surprise when smoke billowed from Larry's gun and the nilgai dropped nicely. Larry has a way of making unbelievable shots.

But one of my fondest memories was an Illinois deer hunt. Larry had scored and was standing with me and another friend as our pals put on a drive. A buck ran by, and I managed to drop it with my muzzleloader. When the smoke cleared, Larry casually mentioned in his wonderful Texas drawl, "Good shot. But why didn't ya'll shoot the big one?" as if he was saying, "pass the butter." Unbeknown to me, a big 10-pointer was directly behind the little guy that I tumbled.

Larry's hunting schedule baffles me. I've never figured out how he can pack so much in a year. I doubt there are many other hunter/writers who can maintain his pace. But he does, and he does it well.

One of Larry's greatest attributes is his personality. The man doesn't have a mean bone in his body. I've never heard him say a negative word about anyone, though some might have deserved it. He is all heart, and his warm smile lights up every room.

When Larry speaks, people listen. And they should. He is a master. His name, "Mr. Whitetail," was earned. As a biologist who has survived numerous helicopter wrecks while surveying deer in Texas, he knows about whitetails. And his experience doesn't end at the Texas border, either. Larry has hunted in every region and most states, continually learning and studying deer and other species wherever he hunts.

This book describes many of his adventures, some wild, some not so wild, in a way only Larry can tell it. From bears to moose to deer to kudus, he'll keep you entertained throughout.

I've enjoyed this book from a different perspective than other readers. I can "hear" Larry's soft-spoken voice in every word. But that's not necessary to appreciate this great book. You'll see what I mean when you get into it. And I'll wager you can't put it down until you've read the last page.

Jim Zumbo, Hunting Editor
Outdoor Life Magazine

Chapter 1

Beginning with the Roar

Darkness melted to a grayish, ashen light. Where there had previously been only black, an inky black, my dad and I had penetrated with a carbide lantern less than an hour ago when he dropped me off at my newly built deer stand; now there were mysterious shapes and forms, half-seen in the dim light. Shapes and forms of which I was uncertain, not scared of perhaps, just a bit suspicious. To my left, only about 20 yards away, was something dark and fairly low to the ground and it appeared to be moving. My first thought was "Bear!" yet I knew from the stories told to me by my dad and my maternal grandfather, A.J. Aschenbeck, that black bears had not roamed our part of Texas for about 70 or so years. Still, the dark shape looked mightily like a bear.

The slight northerly breeze brought a chill factor that made the damp southern Texas air feel like the thermometer was hovering near the freezing and I shivered slightly and sunk deeper into the army blanket that I was partially wrapped in. I stared at the dark shape — I just knew had to be a bear! Did it move?

I wished and prayed the moon would rise again. The one my father had described as a hunter's moon, full and bright, shining with an orange tinge. When we left home I had admired it in the western sky, only a few degrees above the horizon. It had looked considerably larger than usual, but now it was gone. During our drive to Stelzig's Place, where we were to hunt on the opening day of the Texas whitetail season, it had sunk out of sight, leaving a darkness illuminated only by our pickup headlights and later by the stars and my dad's acrid smelling carbide light as we walked to my stand.

After helping me up into my cedar tree deer stand, and then handing up my single-shot .22 deer rifle, I had watched as Daddy disappeared into the darkness. "Gotta be in our stands at least an hour before first light," he had explained over a breakfast of home-cured ham and yard eggs prepared by my mother, "so the woods and the deer settle down." A few moments later in total darkness I took my one precious .22 Long Rifle hollow points out of my old army-surplus wool shirt's front pocket. I carefully put it in the chamber and closed the bolt. I was ready!

There was a certain satisfaction in finally being left to hunt on my own, an affirmation of maturity and trust from my dad. After all, I was going on eight years of age! Yet there was also a little anxiety and excitement, which was hard to explain then and even now, many years later. I sat on the narrow cedar limb as quietly as possible listening to the crickets and other morning bugs and my thoughts drifted once again to the shapes that surrounded me. I gripped my .22 rimfire a little more tightly. At least if the dark shape was a bear, I'd have something to defend myself with.

As the opaque light of predawn turned to the

PREVIOUS PAGE:
The author – Larry Weishuhn

The North American white-tailed deer has fascinated wildlife biologist and master hunter Larry Weishuhn since childhood.

translucent light of dawn, I felt a bit sheepish about my imagination. The bear I had been watching mysteriously transformed itself into a low-growing cedar bush. Other shapes and forms of which I had been equally unsure had also thankfully turned out to be nothing but shrubs, bushes and logs. As night moved toward a brighter morning, melodies of birds filled the air. Over toward Grandpa Weishuhn's stock pens could be heard the sound of cattle — cows lowing their displeasure at having had their calves weaned only the day before.

I listened carefully to the many sounds around me, the scurrying of fox squirrels on fallen white and red oak leaves and an armadillo digging for grubs and ants. Several hundred yards away I could hear crows squawking, probably irritating a hawk, owl or possibly one of the gray foxes that seemed to abound in our woods in relatively great numbers that year. Closer by was a ruckus caused by blue jays. Dad had told me to pay attention to such things, because often blue jays and crows foretold of the coming of deer. If one did, I thought, I would be ready.

Larry Weishuhn with his first-ever whitetail, taken November 16, 1961, on opening morning of the Texas whitetail season. The buck was taken with the author's maternal grandfather's 12-gauge, single-shot shotgun. Larry posed for this photograph with his buck in front of Heinsohn's Store in Frelsburg, Texas.

I waited patiently, but the morning passed without so much of a glimpse of a deer. Quite frankly, by the time I heard Dad's whistle, a signal to unload before he came to pick me up, I was ready to go home. During the course of the morning I had heard a couple of shots but they sounded a long way off. I hoped one of them might be my dad, but I doubted it because he had been hunting from his own stand only about 300 yards away from where I had been hidden in the ancient cedar.

Back in the early 1950s white-tailed deer in our part of Texas were relatively rare, primarily because of screwworm flies, whose larval stages devoured living flesh. Any slight scratch and screwworm flies laid their eggs near or in the wound. The results in deer were often fatal, especially in young fawns. Back then you truly had to hunt hard to even see a deer, but the relative lack of deer did not dampen our interest in hunting them. We hunted deer in November and December. The rest of the year my dad hunted 'coons with his pack of well-trained hounds. When permitted, I trailed along behind him and the hounds but it wasn't always easy. My dad loved his hounds and often it seemed was almost at their side when they trailed or chased a 'coon. With my short legs I had a hard time keeping up with him and his hounds. Then he'd have to come back for me. Still, hunting with my dad was always something I looked forward to doing.

I was fortunate, as youngster I spent many days with my maternal grandfather while my dad was working in the oil fields. He wasn't much of a deer hunter — my dad has long told a tale of taking his father-in-law (my granddad) deer hunting and dropping him off at his own favorite stand. When he returned to pick him up about three hours later he found my grandfather sitting next to a roaring fire he had started right under the tree he had been sitting in. While he was not much of a deer hunter, he did love to hunt squirrels and doves, and occasionally shot a duck on the clear-flowing Cummins Creek which meandered along the edge of his property only a couple hundred yards from his home. The site had long been a favorite camping place for hunters, as evidenced by the arrowheads and other Indian arti-

Larry with the mount of his late season 1963 fork-horned buck. Taken from a tree stand with his father's rifle, the buck was the reward of a long and hard hunt.

facts we often found there when I was a youngster.

"Fotta," as his grandchildren called him, was partial to an old single-shot 12-gauge shotgun. He affectionately referred to it as "The Roar." To say he was deadly on squirrels and flying mourning doves with the old "single-barrel" would have been an understatement, I never remember him missing a shot. I don't recall the first time I shot the old 12-gauge. It had to have been quite an occasion. Strangely too, I do not remember my first hunts. Perhaps it's because my dad and granddad started taking me hunting when I was still in diapers, carrying me in their arms while they hunted squirrels.

When I was not working or being forced to go to school, I hunted. Each evening I had my mother read to me from the pages of *Outdoor Life*, *Sports Afield* and any other hunting magazine I could get my hands on. Quite frankly when I started to attend school, I thought I was being punished and had been sent directly to hell! When I finally learned to read I devoted any money I earned from chores — money not spent on .22 Short and .22 Long Rifle shells — to the purchase of the latest issues of various hunting and gun magazines that, back then, cost about 25 to 35 centsper issue.

I lived to hunt and occasionally fish. I spent most of my early childhood in the woods and fields around our rural home. Back then our neighbors did not look suspiciously at a red-haired youngster walking through their woods carrying a .22 rifle. Prior to being allowed to roam on my own, my dad, mother and grandparents instilled gun safety in me. I knew that if I made any sort of mistake or improper use of a firearm, I would have lost that privilege and I held that privilege sacred! I was not about to do anything wrong! Gun ownership might have been a guaranteed right for Americans, but in my youth it was also a privilege — one that, if I misbehaved, would swiftly be revoked!

As I grew older, my deer hunting interest increased annually in a downright fever. As a pre-teen I dreamed of hunting with a real deer gun and drooled over my dad's Model 94 Winchester, .30-30. If I had a gun like that, I thought, I would be a true deer hunter! I might not have been able to tell you anything about the school lessons and homework I had done but I could quote chapter and verse about deer guns, giving the precise ballistics and gun writers' assessments.

By the fall of 1961 I was a veteran deer hunter, with no less than six hunting-in-the-stand-by-myself years of experience, but I had not yet been able to take my first deer. It wasn't for a lack of interest, nor time spent in the deer stand or, for that matter, preseason scouting. I had spent many hours in the woods, learning how to read sign, interpreting it, looking for shed antlers. I read about deer hunting and pestered any and all of the successful deer hunters with whom I came in contact with a seemingly endless string of questions. When not hunting, I spent a considerable amount of time roaming the woods behind our home, looking for treasure. My greatest treasure and "best medicine" were shed antlers and the spent cartridges used by others to kill whitetails. Surely such great medicine would bring me success.

With the coming of the 1961 season and my still not having my truly own deer gun, my mom and dad suggested I use "Fotta's" 12 gauge, "the

Roar"; perhaps his gun would bring me the luck I desired. "Fotta" Aschenbeck had passed away when I was nine. During my early childhood he had made a tremendous impression upon me, taught me about hunting and fishing, taught me about guns and in his own way had taught me about myself.

He has remained a tremendous influence in my life but for a while that influence was "strained" a bit. It's taken me years to admit it to myself, but when he died I got and stayed mad at him for quite a while. I blamed him for dying, because I missed him so horribly. But then finally I started realizing how important he had been to me, and how his death dying of lung cancer, had not been his fault and it had been wrong for me to blame him.

When Mama and Daddy suggested that I use my grandfather's gun, I wondered why I had not thought of doing so earlier. A quick call to my uncle who had inherited the old shotgun assured me that I would be able to use it, and he would drop it by the house the next time he headed over our way, which was usually about once a week.

That year before the opening of hunting season, Daddy gave me three 12-gauge Remington double-ought buck shells. At a makeshift range in the back of our pasture I pulled the "Roar's" trigger at a hand-drawn target of a deer. At 30 yards I put a sufficient number of buckshot into the "kill zone" to be certain I could kill a deer with the combination, provided the range was not much farther than the distance to the target.

Well before the opening of hunting season, Daddy, Mama and I all built stands in the woods behind our house on the Paasch land. The Paasch family's property bordered our's on two sides. To pay for our hunting rights on their property Daddy and I helped them work cattle and haul hay, something when you got right down to it we would have done anyway because they were neighbors. Permission was given when we asked about hunting; as additional payment they asked to have some venison should we be so fortunate as to take a deer.

My stand was an old leaning oak which overlooked a small intermittent creek. Boards were nailed into the trunk to form steps. Then high in the tree, about 30 feet above the ground in a convenient fork, Daddy and I nailed a couple of boards that would serve as a seat and backrest.

Days passed slower than those before Christmas or the nearing end of school as I waited for opening day of the deer season. November 16 was back

then Texas' traditional opening day. And thank goodness as luck would have it that year opening day fell on a Saturday, otherwise I would have missed school. I was not about to miss opening day of deer season for anything!

Way before first light, at least two hours before, I was already sitting in my stand. As memory serves me, it took at least a full year, a leap year at that, for those two hours to pass and for it to get light enough to see anything. Long before the official half-hour before the legal sunup shooting hour I had become attuned to every single sound and move made by leaf, bird, squirrel and even insect. There was no doubt when the precise appointed moment of the opening of hunting season arrived, for off in the distance could be heard several shots, and then some a bit closer.

Hope and anticipation probably lead to several small prayers being uttered. About the time I was mentally uttering an "Amen" I heard a shot I knew had come from the direction where Daddy was hunting. Dad seldom missed so I felt good about the possibility that he had a deer down.

Before I even had a chance to wonder how many points Dad's buck might have, I heard something running my way. At first I thought it might simply be a squirrel, but it was far too loud for a squirrel. I looked to the west and there coming through the yaupon bushes next to the little creek came what I perceived as being the new world record whitetail! And he was coming my way. With any luck he would pass nearly under my tree stand. My muscles tensed and my hands and knees started shaking. I sat transfixed, watching the monster deer quickly entering the area where I had marked my 30-yard distance.

I scarcely remember bringing the shotgun to my shoulder and peering down the barrel as I tried to align the notched receiver with the steel bead at the muzzle's end. He was monstrous and he was my chance not only to take my first deer, but gain fame and immortality as well!

The buck came onward moving almost directly under and slightly in front of my stand and still I had not taken my shot. My hands, holding the old 12 gauge, shook, my knees shook, quite likely the entire tree shook. Thankfully the buck had slowed to a walk and now it looked as if he was about to stop and turn to watch his back trail.

The "Roar's" front bead seemed to line up with the back notch right upon the buck's shoulder.

Now, pull the trigger! I pulled but nothing happened, thousands of "Oh My God . . . What's Going Wrong Now" thoughts pinged through my mind. Thankfully, about then, before the buck-of-all-bucks moved, I realized I had forgotten to pull back the hammer. Reaching up I cocked the old single-barrel's hammer. The sound seemed so loud that surely every deer in the woods would hear it.

I looked back down at the buck, praise of all praise he was still there, looking at his back trail. Again kingdoms rose to power and fell into ruin before I again got the bead, the back notch and the buck's shoulder all lined up in the same plain.

"Take a deep breath before pulling the trigger!" I remembered reading, the advice of an experienced deer hunter in some hunting magazine. I heeded his advice and gulped some air. In so doing, the bead sight and the notch again failed to align properly with the buck's shoulder. Quickly I readjusted.

All looked in proper alignment, I tugged at the trigger and felt the "Roar" recoil. That recoil, even though I was big for my age, pushed me backwards and I momentarily lost sight of the buck. Frantic I looked where he had stood, the buck-of-all-bucks was lying on the ground, but he was stirring and trying to gather his feet underneath him.

"He's gonna get up!" I spoke out loud, while remembering at the same time that I had another shell. While fishing it out of my pocket, I looked down and saw the buck-of-all-bucks rise to his feet and start wobbly walking away from where he had fallen. That truly put me into a panic!

With great strength I broke open the old shotgun, to replace the spent shell. But in so doing I just happened to tug a bit too much on the forearm, which came loose in my left hand. As the laws of physics state, "for every action there is a reaction," in this situation the reaction was, when the forend was removed the barrel disengaged from the action. I sat there in horror as I watched as the barrel of my shotgun started falling to the soft ground some 30 feet below my stand. It fell in slow motion; buck fawns were conceived, born, weaned grew numerous, many grew great racks and died of old age, before the barrel stuck into the ground below. There I sat 30 feet high in a tree, with the buttstock of the old shotgun in one hand, the forend in the other, a 12-gauge buckshot load clenched tightly in my mouth, where I had placed it so I wouldn't drop it while unloading and reloading the "Roar." Life was not good at the moment!

For a brief moment I seriously considered jumping out of my tree to recover it. Thankfully I didn't! As I looked at the barrel and wondered what I would do next, I happened to look in the direction of where my buck-of-all-bucks had staggered and watched as the last part of him disappeared into the brush. Finally and thankfully some reasoning ability returned to my buck-fever wrecked body and I decided to crawl down from my tree stand and then regather my gun parts and pursue the most "awesome" buck of all times.

As I remember, I more slid down the tree and ran to where my shotgun barrel was stuck into the ground, muzzle first. I pulled it out of the mud, and unbelievably had the forethought to blow the mud out of the end of the barrel, reassemble my shotgun and stoke in the fresh double-ought buckshot shell into its chamber.

That chore completed, although not nearly as cleanly nor as easily as described, I turned and headed to where I had last seen my buck disappear into the yaupon thicket. Immediately I spotted a few flecks of blood and was so intently looking for more as I walked a few steps forward that I nearly tripped on the dead deer practically under my feet. My buck! I let out a yell that my dad later described as somewhat of a cross between a hoop, holler, and a high-pitched scream. Years later he told me he's never before or since heard a human being make a noise of its equal!

Before even looking at what I knew would be the new world record rack, I mumbled a prayer of thanks, not only to the Almighty but also to "Fotta" and his old shotgun. Slowly my eyes started moving toward the buck's head.

Much to my surprise, where I had seen, identified and knew that there would be the antlers belonging to the new world record whitetail and

the most important deer of all times, there were two spikes, one about 6 inches long, the other about 4 inches. There was no doubt, even though he may have only had spikes, he was still THE MOST IMPORTANT DEER OF ALL TIMES!

For about 10 minutes I simply sat at my buck's side marveling at his majesty, recalling the many hours I had previously hunted waiting, hoping and dreaming of this moment when I made the transition from being a deer hunter to a successful deer hunter who had taken his first deer! My mind drifted in many directions, recalling times with my dad sitting in a tree stand next to him, walking the woods learning from Daddy and Fotta about reading and interpreting deer sign, listening totally enthralled to my parents' friends talking about their deer hunting experiences. There were no words to describe my feelings. There still aren't!

Today a shoddy neck mount of that buck resides upon my office wall. Few who see it realize the importance of that particular buck, and likely some scoff at his size, or wonder why someone who has pursued the hunter's moon throughout the world would bother to have that buck mounted, and with many other bigger racks to his credit would have it in such a place of honor?

What is important is that each time I look up at that little whitetail mount, I recall the feeling I felt sitting there at its side soon after it died. Looking at it I recall the sounds of the morning. I remember the shot I had heard in the distance which had been fired by my dad at one of the few bucks he's ever missed and knowing now there was a reason for his doing so. I recall the smell of the smoke of the gunpowder from the old shotgun. I vividly remember the aromas of the morning before and after I became a successful deer hunter and thinking of Fotta, knowing somewhere in the great beyond he watched with a smile as his grandson used his "Roar" to take his first deer.

Larry Weishuhn poses with his first 8-point buck, taken on the back part of his childhood home in northern Colorado County, Texas. His rifle is a re-stocked .257 Roberts.

CHAPTER 2

EARLY
WHITETAILS

The oak, cedar and yaupon woods behind our house formed a haven for white-tailed deer and times were good. Screwworm flies had been eradicated in our part of Texas thanks to modern science and the state's aggressive approach to controlling this flesh-eating pest. Deer herds that could at best have been described as "meager" only three years earlier were now flourishing and populations were fast reaching the range's carrying capacity. But for someone totally enamored with deer there was no such thing as "too many." Many of the ranchers in our area and all the deer hunters agreed, "Too many deer? No way!"

We looked at it as a fortuitous situation — one we had longed for and dreamed of experiencing. A few years later as a trained wildlife biologist with a degree in Wildlife Management from Texas A&M University, I would see the errors in my thoughts about deer populations. But that was later. For the time being deer hunting was good! For someone who recalled sitting in the woods most of the deer season without ever seeing more than three or four deer all season long, seeing as many as 20 or more deer in a day seemed like heaven.

For the most part the local deer population was young and growing. Fairly heavy hunting pressure seldom allowed bucks to mature and most were shot as yearlings and two-year-olds. Occasionally, someone would shoot a sizable 8- or 10-pointer. And, when they did, both hunter and deer were celebrated. Those young bucks were good teachers. I well remember the lessons learned from one particular fork-horn, a big buck in the woods behind our house. I spotted him one afternoon a few days before the opening of deer season. He was feeding on freshly fallen Spanish oak acorns just beyond our fence in the Fahrenkampt pasture.

A cool wind blew out of the east and by taking advantage of it, keeping the sun at my back and staying hidden behind some tall grass cover, I was able to slip quietly to within about 15 yards of where he fed without him even suspecting my presence. Back then, no one in our part of the country, save few city people, used binoculars, and telescopic rifle sights were things only read about in the pages of *Outdoor Life* and *Sports Afield*. So regardless of whether you were hunting or scouting, to get a really good look at a deer you had to get close and rely on woodsmanship, which most of us equated to taking advantage of the wind blowing or quartering into your face, keeping the sun at your back, moving with extreme caution only when the animal was looking the other way and taking full advantage of cover. Camouflage clothing was practically nonexistent in those days. Hunters simply wore green, brown or gray clothing and occasionally red or green plaids.

The fork-horned buck had an antler spread that just about reached the outside of his forward and erect ears. He lacked brow tines and his antlers were rubbed slick to the point of being shiny. I watched as the buck fed for a good 20 minutes under an old Spanish oak. Occasionally he would raise his head and look around. Usually when he did, his nostrils would flare slightly as he interpreted the scents drifting upon the wind. When satisfied no danger was present he would again begin feeding on the acorns.

PREVIOUS PAGE:
A youthful Larry Weishuhn poses behind his house with a forkhorn buck that he took late in the 1963 Texas deer season. Larry shot the buck with his father's "thutty-thutty" rifle while sitting in his father's favorite deer stand, a place that seemed to be a buck magnet.

This 19-inch-wide 10-point buck responded to rattling on the Davis Ranch just southwest of Abilene, Texas, in December 1975. After being told that bucks would not respond to rattling antlers in that area, Larry rattled up and took the buck. That same afternoon he rattled up and shot a second 10-pointer.

I noticed this buck was a bit different than others I had observed behind the house. His hair was rather long. Most of the deer in our area, even going into the fall, tended to have a rather sleek looking hair coat. This one was different. My dad had always taught me to be observant, to notice the little things. As a small youngster we would either ride horseback or walk through a herd of cattle and he would point out those with the slightest abnormalities or health problems. In so doing he taught me to look for the little things and taught me to be observant not only of animals and their surroundings. Those early teachings have paid off handsomely many, many times during my years in the deer woods and game fields.

Finally the young buck, likely a two-year-old, ate his fill and disappeared into the wolf-weeds and nearby thicket of yaupon and greenbrier. After he left I walked under the big oak, picked up some acorns and put them into my pocket. Later I would add them to my "medicine bag," a Bull Durham tobacco sack that had been given to me by my great-grandfather.

I did not see the buck again until about a week into the hunting season. Until then I had assumed he had either left our area, or perhaps had roamed a few pas-

tures over and gotten shot. That particular morning I was sitting in Daddy's deer stand, near the center of the property we hunted. Next to the tree that my dad normally hunted from was a little "flat" that held water during wet times. It seemed that, for some reason, this was a "buck crossing." If there was a buck living in the area, or even if one just passed through, he would inevitably pass by my dad's deer stand. We never did determine the reason for this, but simply accepted the fact and took advantage of this natural "buck trail."

It was cold that morning. I shivered a bit and was thankful for the brown-duck, brush popper jacket I wore. Dad had always told me that when I was hunting I should to try to smell as much as possible like something deer were used to smelling. The afternoon before, I had worn the old brown-duck jacket while working cattle and I can assure you that it smelled more of cattle than most cows did. The deer in our area were accustomed to smelling cows.

The morning passed slowly, but I was entertained by blue jays fussing at a gray fox, and then crows chasing an owl which had lingered a bit too long before returning home before first light. I was watching a squirrel bury an acorn when I heard something walking behind me and to my left. I turned and at the same time brought Daddy's Model 94 .30-30, which in those days wore a Weaver K4 scope on a side-mount, to my right shoulder.

I immediately recognized the deer. It was the big, shiny-horned fork-horn I had seen before the season opened. He was walking fairly quickly and before I could get him in my sights he moved directly behind me. Hurriedly I swung around with the rifle mounted on my right shoulder, but try as I might, I could not turn far enough around to get him in my sights before he disappeared.

I was disgusted with myself. I had seen the buck I dearly wanted to take that year and yet I had failed when the opportunity presented itself. I thought about it for a while and what I could have done differently. Then it hit me. Had I been able to shoot accurately from my left-hand side, there might well have been an opportunity to take the buck. Even though there was still hunting time left, I immediately tied the Model 94 to the end of the safety string used to pull up and lower my rifle from the stand, then lowered the "thutty-thutty" to the ground. I hurriedly climbed down the wooden ladder nailed to the tree, untied the rifle, slung it over my shoulder and headed home.

No one was at the house when I got there so I properly stowed the .30-30, grabbed my old single-shot Remington .22 rimfire, a box of shells and, on my way to the terraces below the windmill and the stock pens, I grabbed a couple of empty tomato cans out of the trash barrel.

After setting up the cans and then making certain that any errant bullets would not cause harm to anything beyond, I started teaching myself to shoot left-handed. It took a bit of doing, but after about 10 minutes of practice I was hitting a tomato can set out at about 20 steps using my new left-hand shooting stance. I left the morning's shooting session convinced that if ever again I was presented with a left-hand shot, I'd be able to make it.

Interestingly, the chance to test my left-hand shooting ability came during the Christmas holidays. Daddy had already taken his two bucks that year, one on opening day and the other the day after Thanksgiving. Thus I was allowed to use his deer rifle and hunt out of his stand!

Morning broke with a cold wind blowing out of the north and the temperature hovering near freezing. I did my best to hug the south side of my dad's tree so it would block the wind. I'd been in the stand for about an hour when I spotted movement. It was the "big" fork-horn. He was walking the same trail as before and was moving in the same direction at about the same pace.

This time, rather than trying to swing the rifle all the way around on my right side, I simply switched shoulders and was ready for the buck when he reappeared to my right. As soon as the sights settled on his vitals, I gently tugged the trigger. The buck took a few steps and, before I could lever in another 170-grain round, he was down. It took a bit for my good fortune to sink in. But when it did, I let out a whoop that, had it not been for the strong wind blowing, could have been heard back at the house a bit over a mile away. Learning to shoot left-handed had been something of a stroke of genius — or at least so I thought. Actually I still feel that same way, because during many years on hunts throughout North America and elsewhere I have often had to switch hurriedly to my left side to take the animal I was after.

The hunt had not only proven the value of learning how to shoot left-handed, but also the importance of being persistent. Back then, in our part of the country, if you didn't take a deer during the first three days of the season, chances were almost 100 percent you weren't going to be using the buck tag on your hunting license that year. Persistence and hope, as well as a certain amount of faith, paid off handsomely for me that year. Many times since, it's come down to the last moment of a hunt to take the animal I was after. Had I given up earlier, those hunts would not have been successful in terms of taking game.

Lessons of the school variety were a different matter and had always been a challenge for me, especially in the fall. My grades during the spring were good, but not so when the first cool breezes of fall started blowing, bringing with them the promise that deer season was soon to follow. This was the case not only in high school and before, but also when I enrolled in college.

During the latter part of high school I met the young lady I knew I wanted to spend the rest of my life with. We were married when we were both 19 years old, just before the beginning of my sophomore year in college — a decision that I have never regretted! If I had to do it all over again, it is definitely one of the things I'd not change. Quite frankly, had it not been for her, I would never have gone on to do what I've done in life.

Nearly every day while I was attending Texas A&M University, especially during the fall, I'd come home from classes and tell her to pack up, that I was sick and tired of college and that we were leaving. Somehow she'd talk me out of quitting. And she kept doing so until I finally got a degree.

During our first years of marriage, hunting played a different role than it had before we were married. I now hunted deer so we'd have meat on the table. Even after I graduated from college and started a career as a wildlife biologist, hunting remained important to provide meat for our young family, which by then included our daughter, Theresa. Not long after Theresa, came our other daughter, Elizabeth. Back then a wildlife biologist's salary provided just about enough money to pay the rent and buy staples. Meat, unless harvested from the wild, was a luxury.

I was extremely fortunate that in my senior year I went to work for the Texas

Mustached, the author with a 10-point buck he took on the McGahee Ranch southwest of Abilene, Texas, back in 1976, using a Remington Model 700 .270 Winchester.

Wildlife Disease Project headed up by Dr. R.M. Robinson, working as an undergraduate assisting in all sorts of wildlife research. Immediately after graduation I signed on as the research technician in charge of various projects and studies. Our project, back in the early 1970s, was charged not only with performing wildlife disease research, but also with wildlife nutrition research, especially focusing on white-tailed deer. My work there opened a brand-new world in more ways than one. Three years after signing on with the project, I was hired by the Texas Parks & Wildlife Department and assigned to work statewide on the Wildlife Disease Project and other deer research.

At that time biologists Al Brothers and Murphy Ray were just beginning to form some of their theories on quality deer management. Fortunately, we were not only able to support their theories with research, but also develop some of the basic techniques of quality management. At about the same time, John Wootters, who later became my mentor and close friend, was just starting to write about the value of hunting mature deer. His articles were illustrated by photographs taken by fellow Texan Jerry Smith, to show the public what whitetail bucks could look like if given the opportunity to mature.

A few years later during the beginning of outdoor videos, I often worked with Jerry Smith to produce some extremely high-quality hunting and management videos. Probably the most popular one we did, and one that continues to survive today, was one John Wootters and I collaborated on about field-judging and field-aging whitetail bucks. I am told it has become a true classic, one that is still purchased and used in many, many hunting camps.

The early and mid-1970s were the opening years of whitetail hunting as we have come to know them today. I was extremely fortunate to have been around and involved in those early years and to have continued in all the whitetail management and hunting fields since then.

As biologists involved in deer research, we spent considerable time in the field, not only observing deer but also collecting them for a wide variety of study. Every deer shot, and we shot many with a wide variety of firearms and occasionally even archery equipment, were necropsied (the animal term for autopsy). Each and every organ of every deer was checked and samples were taken for histology work and blood values. Quite often, rumen content samples were taken to determine what the deer were eating and then later taken to the laboratory to determine the rumen content's total protein, calcium and phosphorous values. Back then our equipment was not nearly as sophisticated as it is today, but even so, we collected a considerable amount of baseline data relative to deer health and nutrition.

During those years I essentially hunted for a living when not overseeing

John Wootters poses with the author in the South Texas scrub. Wootters' writings on whitetail population management, particularly the harvesting of mature bucks, were a major influence in modern quality deer management.

This interesting Texas Brush
Country buck was killed just north
of Laredo during the waning days
of hunting season.

research with our penned deer on the Texas A&M campus or working statewide. We shot a tremendous number of deer throughout the state of Texas in every conceivable good to marginal deer habitat. Procuring "samples" quite often came down to employing our best deer hunting techniques. In the process I had great opportunities to learn about deer habit, what and when they ate, where and how they lived. And also, because we were shooting enough of them, I had the opportunity to learn about terminal performance of bullets and shot placement.

What did I do when there was any free time, of which there admittedly was very little? I hunted white-tailed deer and, when time permitted, other species including some of the exotic deer that made their home in Texas. I also chased mule deer on occasion. Every now and then I'd shoot something big enough to warrant putting it on the wall, but mostly I hunted for venison to feed my young family.

Unfortunately political problems and lack of funding brought a halt to our Wildlife Disease Project. Most of the white-tailed deer we kept in our research facility at Texas A&M University were moved to the Spike Deer and Nutrition research project recently begun on Texas' Kerr Wildlife Management Area. When our project folded, my family and I moved to northwestern Texas, where I continued working as a wildlife biologist covering the management of numerous species on a considerable portion in that part of the state. It was while living in Abilene that I reached new conclusions about hunting whitetails. A new hunter's moon was about to rise!

During most of my life as a deer hunter I had generally taken the first legal buck I had a chance to shoot. Slowly, my thoughts about whitetails began to change because I was now aware of what could happen to antlers and body size if bucks were just given the opportunity to mature. Antlers, I had learned, were beyond doubt the result of age, nutrition and genetics. Over much of Texas, as well as in most of North America, whitetails seldom had the opportunity to mature, much less to mature in the presence of good daily nutrition and rarely came close to achieving their genetic potential for body and antler development. Perhaps I had spent too much time listening to Al Brothers, Murphy Ray and Dr. R.M. Robinson, and reading John Wootters' magazine articles and looking at Jerry Smith's photos. Yet, at the same time, due to the research I had been involved in, I knew they were right. After all, I had also helped develop several of the quality whitetail management techniques they suggested in their writings and seminars. Practice what you preach!

My thoughts on hunting deer changed dramatically one afternoon on a bushy, shin oak and brush-covered ridge southwest of Abilene, Texas. I had gotten permission to hunt deer on the property in exchange for several days of helping the owner work his cattle. During one of those cattle working days on horseback, I had jumped a sizable buck in the canyon where I planned to hunt.

A fierce north wind, carrying occasional snow flurries, blew that afternoon as I eased slowly into the canyon. I had just started into the canyon mouth when I saw a buck walking on the opposite slope. Quickly, the .270 Winchester I carried came to my shoulder and just as quickly I found a solid rest in the fork of a nearby persimmon tree. The crosshairs floated all over the deer and then settled nicely on his shoulder. I touched the trigger and saw the deer fall.

After marking the spot just below a lightning-struck, dead oak, I headed across the narrow canyon toward the fallen deer, believing that I had taken the deer I had seen a couple of weeks earlier. As I neared the dead deer, I noticed his antlers were not the same as those of the buck I had seen earlier. I knelt at his side and counted 9 short points on his rather narrow, spindly-weight rack, then held his head to open his mouth to age him, the benefit of years of working as a wildlife biologist specializing in white-tailed deer. Immediately, I saw the three cusps of the third pre-molar, confirmation that the deer was only about 18 months of age — a yearling.

The joy and excitement I had experienced while walking toward my deer was suddenly gone, and I dearly wished I could turn back the hands of time, hold my shot, and allow this young buck to walk away. Had I not taken that deer, he might have developed into a buck with a truly monstrous rack of antlers.

I had not taken the deer because I needed venison to feed my family, since there was plenty of opportunity to shoot does. There was no real reason to take that young buck and I was greatly dissatisfied with myself. At that moment I resolved to never again shoot an immature buck, unless it was as part of an overall management program to keep a herd within a habitat's carrying capacity. Over the years I've kept that promise to myself and to that deer, of not shooting bucks which have not yet reached maturity, at least three years of age or older, and primarily those considerably older.

It was at about this stage in my career, as both a wildlife biologist and a hunter, that I started learning that mature deer are a completely different animal. And if you plan on taking a mature buck, you'd better change your hunting ways and attitudes about deer.

With my new resolve to pursue only mature deer, I truly started getting a whitetail education! In later years that education lead to my writing a book titled *Hunting Mature Bucks*, and to be honest, that education continues every time I head into the deer woods.

Larry back in the late 1970s, when he frequently hunted whitetails in northern Mexico, a bit hairier then, but so were some of his Mexican hunting experiences.

CHAPTER 3

LURE OF CACTUS
AND
THORN

T hings have changed quite a bit since I first came down this way," said Al Brothers, biologist for the Zachary Ranches of South Texas, as he pointed to a massive, multipointed and dark antlered whitetail buck mount hanging on his office wall. "To begin with, there were fewer deer. Between the screwworms and predators, the deer populations were suppressed. But there was always plenty to eat, bucks matured and grew sizable antlers." He continued, "Now deer populations are on the increase, but so is hunting pressure, especially on bucks, and on many ranches they don't have the opportunity to mature and grow antlers like that one."

After looking at several more of Al's impressive mounts — bucks he had taken not only in South Texas, but also in Oklahoma during his stint with military service — he suggested we go to town, Laredo, and have lunch with Murphy Ray. Murphy, at the time, was a wildlife biologist with the Texas Parks & Wildlife Department. Although they had discussed the idea of a book about deer management, it wasn't until about five years later that Al and Murphy wrote *Producing Quality Whitetails*, a book that has become the bible for those interested in producing better quality deer on the properties they own, manage or hunt.

Over lunch we discussed several research projects dealing with deer nutrition and habitat management that Al, Murphy and a few others were jointly involved in at the time. The discussion was a good one, but not the most important thing to happen that day. Late that afternoon I shot my first deer in South Texas, the famed thorn and cactus Mecca for white-tailed deer hunters. Starting in the early 1970s and even before, every deer hunter I met, be they Texan or "forrinners" had the same dream, to hunt the *muy grande* whitetails of the South Texas Brush Country. I was certainly no different. Like them I had heard tales, read magazine articles, and seen photos and mounts of monster whitetails that had been taken in the famous "Brush Country of South Texas."

The trip to meet with Al and Murphy was something of a dream come true and, to put it mildly, I was so excited to finally get to experience the Brush Country I could scarcely contain myself. With lunch finished, we headed to one of the ranches that Al Brothers managed where he and Murphy had started a quality management program and were just now reaching the time where they should begin to see the results of their efforts.

Just before dark, two deer appeared at the edge of the sendero, a narrow lane cut through the brush, that we were sitting on — one a cautious slick-headed old doe and the other, a love-sick monster buck with 12 long typical points and a spread that would require both of the size-13 Justin boots I was wearing placed heel-to-toe to measure. My heart raced, my palms started sweating and I shook considerably as I raised my .270 rifle and peered through the scope. I identified the target, centered the crosshairs on the deer's shoulder, and then gently tugged at the trigger.

"Good shot!" came Murphy Ray's voice from behind me. And honestly, I swelled a bit with pride. The deer had gone down immediately with the shot. But just in case there was movement, I bolted-in another round and started toward the downed deer. As we walked to her side — "Her side?" you

PREVIOUS PAGES: Flanked by prickly pear cactus, J. Wayne Fears (left) supports his buck assisted by Larry Weishuhn. Fears took this whitetail on one of the many ranches the author managed at the time.

A big 8-point buck runs from a helicopter during a game survey in southern Texas. In the course of his duties as a wildlife biologist, the author spent considerable time conducting helicopter surveys of deer herds to gather information for wildlife management recommendations.

ask – I made certain she was dead and then pulled out my rubber gloves and sharp knife to began the process of eviscerating and taking all the appropriate samples for our research project. "He's still standing there not sure of what's happened," commented Murphy about the true *muy grande* that stood only about a hundred yards away to observe what we were doing.

At that time the ranch we were on was in an area of South Texas that did not allow the legal killing of does, but I could take does due to a collection permit I held from the game department to conduct research. At the time we were involved in a reproduction and nutrition study and shot nothing but does. Thus, we got what scientific data and information we needed, and Al and the ranch got does removed, which was badly needed, a good combination.

During my first years of hunting the South Texas Brush Country I concentrated on taking does for several research projects involving deer nutrition, reproduction, parasite and disease problems. In the process we learned a considerable amount about white-tailed deer, and in time, due to our efforts things began to change in South Texas. In the early 1970s practically no does were taken in southern Texas, but today there are generally more does than bucks killed each hunting season.

My first opportunity to take a buck in South Texas happened years after I shot my first doe there. I had just recently replaced Murphy Ray as the Texas Parks & Wildlife Department technical assistance biologist for the South Texas region. The job of a technical assistance biologist was to work with landowners, managers and hunters on a one-on-one basis, to help them establish quality management programs on their property. It was a job that I dearly loved.

Starting in the late summer and continuing on until the opening of hunting season, I spent nearly every daylight hour in a helicopter, conducting game surveys in an effort to determine the deer herd density and composition on many properties. I also took a look at the habitat to develop workable quality game management plans and programs on particular properties. The helicopter not only proved to be a valuable tool to help take a census of the deer

Dressed for cold weather, Larry Weishuhn wipes down the action of his rifle in the deer camp where he started hunting as a boy. The camp was located only a few hundred yards behind his family home in the Zimmerscheidt community of Texas.

Rattling horns during the late pre-rut and rut to imitate the sound of challenges between rival bucks can generate considerable excitement on a hunt. Horn rattling is the best way to attract a buck during the rut.

herds, it also acted as a highly mobile platform to view property. I could learn more about a ranch in a couple of hours of flying over it in a helicopter than I could have in a year spending all my time on the ground. The helicopter proved a highly effective tool, but they don't always stay in the air.

Over the nearly 20 years I spent in them, we had several mishaps, but thankfully none has proven as devastating as the crash in which Al Brothers was paralyzed from his waist on down. In reflecting on the many times I ended up unintentionally riding one of those contraptions to the ground, and the fact that other friends — helicopter pilots — lost their lives in crashes, certainly makes my mishaps seem far less significant. Even so, the helicopter, especially in South Texas, remains a highly effective management tool.

My first South Texas buck, a really nice 10-pointer with about an 18-inch spread, came to my rattling horns one dark, foggy mid-December morning. The fog made him look much bigger than he actually was and by the time the buck stopped no less than 10 steps in front of me, I was a nervous wreck. Remembering how excited I was and how badly I was shaking, it surprises me I even hit him.

During my years of being involved as a biologist in numerous research projects in South Texas, I had on numerous occasions rattled up bucks, some simply for the pure joy of doing so, and others while guiding hunters on the properties we had set up for research. Those rattling bouts had been exciting, but not nearly like rattling up a buck when I had a gun in my hand.

Working in South Texas I sometimes had the opportunity to fly over the property I would later hunt. Occasionally I would pick out a buck that I had seen during a helicopter game survey to hunt, and I'd hunt that buck to the exclusion of all others. That may sound like making things a bit easy, but you might be surprised. Over the years while doing surveys I saw hundreds of thousands of deer, including numerous outstanding bucks. Interestingly, during the time I kept records of such things, less than one-tenth of one percent of the big bucks I saw while doing these surveys were ever taken by hunters. That will give you some idea as to how many of the bucks I observed from the air I took while hunting several weeks later.

For a while I hunted a 14,000-acre ranch north and slightly east of Laredo, which was owned by the LaMantia family. I got to be good friends with them and had a standing invitation to hunt the ranch when time permitted. And I made certain that was often. One year during a helicopter survey, Greg LaMantia and I spotted an extremely wide 10-pointer with a huge food impaction on his lower left jaw. His antler spread was possibly 28 inches or better, and he appeared to be an old buck, based on body confirmation and overall size. Both Greg and I decided to hunt him, and hunt him we did, for the entire hunting season and the next as well.

Try as we might, and do as we might, we never saw that buck during legal shooting hours. We did see him one night when he ran across the pasture road in front of us, but that was the only time we saw him outside of the game survey. We saw him from the air four years. He was never taken, or, if he was it was by a coyote or the local cougar that, based on the skulls we found of the bucks he killed, was certainly better at hunting and taking old mature whitetails than we were.

The Catorce Ranch, as the LaMantia family called it, provided an interesting study in deer, and over the years produced some extremely good bucks. I did eventually take one of the bucks I had seen earlier that year from the helicopter. He was an old 10-pointer, albeit not all that great in the antler department. In his prime he would likely have been quite a deer, but by the time I took him, probably as a 9-year-old, he had declined quite a bit. I started chasing him early in the season, in mid-November and every opportunity I had, I returned to the ranch to hunt him. Juan, the local vaquero, kept tabs on the deer for me. Each time I got to the ranch, I stopped at the house to check with Juan if he had seen the *dias punta veijo*, and he'd tell me where.

Dutifully I'd head to that part of the ranch. I hunted him by rattling, trying to bait him with corn, still-hunting, sitting in a highly mobile tripod, every conceivable and legal method I could think of! But nary a glimpse did I see of that old buck. I was starting to wonder if Juan was giving me false information!

Then one day I stopped at Juan's house, dropped off a pound of coffee and some sugar and started grilling Juan as to where he saw the old buck and under what circumstances. Then his story broke. Normally Juan would see the deer in an area that I had been hunting while he was driving through the pastures to check on water and cattle. It seemed that whenever Juan drove by near where I had set up a tripod, *el Viejo* would step out to take a look. Hmmmm. With that I started

A *muy grande* whitetail buck vanishes into the vegetation of South Texas' famed Brush Country. Thorny brush, including mesquite, acacia, prickly pear, and mimosa, alternates with grasslands giving the Brush Country the greatest diversity of animal life in Texas.

driving the pasture in my pickup, like Juan had suggested (it's legal to hunt out of a vehicle on private land in Texas). But my driving produced nothing but whitetails disappearing over cactus and bush.

That afternoon I set up in a different area near where I had frequently seen several does, thinking perhaps that the buck might be lured into the open by the attraction of female companionship. Hey! I told you he was old, he wasn't dead! But even the does that afternoon did not warrant his attention. But I did learn something else, especially about Juan's driving through the pastures checking on the cattle. He drove a dilapidated old pickup that made a tremendous clanging noise as it rolled over the rough roads. I also learned something else; the one thing that worked best on Juan's pickup was his radio which was tuned in to the local mariachi station, and Juan had it turned up as loud as was possible. He also sang along to the tunes he knew, and I suspect he knew them all. Ah hah! Finally a revelation in how I might be able to take the buck I had been pursuing.

Next morning I lingered around camp until it was good light. At this time I located three 5-gallon cans, in which I placed a few rocks. I tied these on a piece of rope to the bumper. Then I found part of an old sheet of tin, punched some holes in one side so I could attach a wire and tie it onto the back of my bumper. Then I turned on my pickup radio, found the local Mexican music station, grabbed my gun and away I went through the pasture where Juan had been seeing "my" buck.

I had been "singing" along with the loud music for about 10 minutes after entering *el Viejo's* pasture when I drove right up on him. He stood staring at my pickup from the middle of a knee-high prickly pear "flat" about 75 yards away. I suspect the last sounds he heard were those that he associated with Juan's pickup, a mariachi band complete with accordion playing loudly on the radio. He fell on the spot. All it took to finally get that old buck was a bit of Aggie ingenuity and a few props. In telling this tale of how I finally bested him, I've had some hunters question whether or not the way I took him was actually a fair chase. To be open about it, I had chased that particular buck for two years and hunted him in every fair chase way I knew! If it was not a "fair chase" then at least he was "fairly chased!"

The reward of hunting the South Texas thorn and cactus country is naturally the deer that reside there. Over the years I've frequently hunted in the brush country of both South Texas and northern Mexico, particularly in the Mexican state of Tamaulipas, which lies just below the Rio Grande. I have also hunted the Mexican states of Nuevo Leon and Coahuila. Once you get past the border crossing, hunting in Mexico is an absolute pleasure. In certain ways it is like taking a step back in time. Many of the ranches have few roads, and quite often hunting there is either done on horseback or by simply walking. I prefer the latter but like to have horses available to help pack out the deer. In a later chapter I'll discuss one of the larger deer I hunted there and the lesson that one taught me, but for now I'd prefer to address more pleasant hunts.

Several years ago I hunted on a ranch about 20 miles below the Rio Grande to the west of Nuevo Laredo. Like most Mexican ranches, it was large and, as mentioned, had very few roads other than those that entered the property and a few that connected with the remote windmills that pumped water to a small number of troughs or ponds used to water the ranch's cattle. On that hunt I borrowed a hunting rifle from the rancher rather than go through the complicated procedure of getting gun permits to take my personal guns into Mexico. This was legal as long as I had a Mexican hunting license, which I did.

Early January is the tail end of the rut in that part of Mexico and I had planned

Whitetails, such as this buck, continue to excite not only the author but millions of other hunters as well. Thanks to habitat improvement and careful population management, whitetails now number more than 20 million in North America.

my hunt to get in on the last few days of serious chasing. Cold weather had set in, something of an oddity in that part of the world, and with it came greatly increased deer activity.

On the first morning out I rattled in six bucks. The smallest of which would have been likely to score in the 120s on the B&C scale, the biggest would probably have scored in the mid-140s. Certainly good deer, but I knew there were much better deer on the ranch. One buck that I rattled up that morning that I wished I had taken, and would have done so had the bag limit not been one deer, was a massive, gnarly beamed 6-pointer. He was only about 16 or 17 inches wide, had probably 8-inch brow tines, and 12-inch back tines. But what was most impressive was his mass. He was easily 6 inches at the base and, uncharacteristically of many Texas subspecies whitetails, maintained that mass almost to the tips of his points. He was undoubtedly an older deer. He responded to the horns very slowly, and when he did come in, he walked with a John-Wayne-like swagger. As evidence of his age he also had a potbelly and the skin on his head and neck looked like he'd purchased a suit that was a good three sizes too big for him! Had there been a two-buck limit I would certainly have taken him. In many ways he reminded me of an old bighorn ram, whose horns were broomed and splintered, indicating that he had likely lived a most interesting life. In retrospect I've kicked myself numerous times for not shooting him.

As the hunt wore on, I rattled up numerous bucks, sometimes as many as three

The prickly pear cactus and thorn bush of the Texas Brush Country, home to whitetails and an occasional rattlesnake, remain one of the best places to hunt big-racked white-tailed deer. The Brush Country supports a mixture of tall mesquite and spiny hackberry brush, and short dense brush. The mixture of cover provides habitat for many near tropical species found in Mexico and other grassland species that range northward.

or four were around me at the same time. Most, however, were mere youngsters, or older bucks with 8 points and spreads of 14 to about 19 inches. It seems I found faults and reasons not to shoot every buck I saw. I was beginning to think that the place was over-loaded with deer and that the big-ger bucks I was looking for were nonexistent. I did, however, see an unbelievable number of deer on that hunt, especially considering that I was hunting in Mexico.

On the last morning of the hunt I decided to hunt around a remote water hole that one of the vaqueros had told me about. To get there I

By hunting at an unexpected time — high noon — the author took this 26-inch-wide, 26-inch main beamed, 8-point buck during the last week of the season in southern Texas. He used a .309 JDJ Thompson/Center Contender handgun.

would have to leave camp at about 3:00 in the morning and walk for about four hours. A pretty tall order, but not if I could find the buck that the ranch hand sus-pected watered there each morning.

Just as there was gray light, I sat down on a small rise overlooking the little water hole. Shortly after I sat down against an ancient rough-barked mesquite, a coyote trotted across the little open area that extended all the way to the water hole. He had scarcely walked into the adjoining cactus thicket when a bobcat stepped out. The cat was a big mature male, looking not unlike a short-tailed jaguar in color, but with a slightly muted shade and rosettes. I watched as he stalked a bird near water's edge. But that morning *el gato del brasada* failed and moments later he trotted off into the maize of thorns.

The first sliver of sun showed over the mesquite-studded horizon, and all around the world was turning to gold. It was the reflection of that golden light bouncing off of the buck's dark mahogany-colored antlers that caught my atten-tion. The moment he began to appear from behind a huge clump of prickly pear, I knew there was no reason to check him out through my binoculars. Up came the rifle, and I panned the scope's crosshairs across his head and rack. A quick glance at his antlers revealed that both the left and right sides were present. There were at least 10 points, albeit not terribly long, but certainly massive. His rack was so mas-sive it almost appeared as a solid blob on the buck's head.

I had seen enough and quickly settled the crosshairs just slightly forward of the buck's shoulder as he walked toward the water hole. The buck fell at the shot, but I didn't see him go down due to the recoil of the .300 H&H Magnum I was shoot-ing. No sooner than I had fired the shot, than I bolted-in another round and start-ed looking for the buck. I saw a horizontal antler tip come up and then go down. I jumped up and walked fast to cover the 125 yards that separated me from the fallen buck. By the time I got there he was dead.

I knelt at his side and marveled at his rack — it was indeed massive! Reaching around the bases with my fingers I estimated them to be at least 6 inches in cir-cumference and he carried that same basic mass throughout the rest of the beam. I counted his points and came up with 14, seven on each side, a basic 5 by 5 with double brow tines and a kicker point on either beam between his brows and the burr. I was still trembling a bit many minutes later when I began the field-dressing and capeing chores. Once the insides and his cape and head were removed, I hung the buck from a nearby mesquite. Back at camp I told the vaquero where the buck was hanging so that he could retrieve him with his horse, as he had volunteered to do. Mexico's land of thorns and spines had paid handsome dividends.

Back on the Texas side of the Rio Grande I also spent many wonderful days afield. And here the word "days" is the keyword indeed. I learned early on that in hunting, the best way to take a deer is to go hunting and to hang in there until the last moment. During my years as a wildlife biologist in southern Texas I learned the value of hunting during midday, a time when most hunters were in camp.

One of my finest bucks, a massive long-tined 8-pointer, with 26-inch main beams and a 26-inch outside spread, fell at almost exactly 12 noon. Actually I was driving from one part of a rather expansive ranch to another, heading for an area where the year before I had seen a truly impressive buck, although one I thought was possibly a year away from being a "shooter."

I was easing along slowly in my vehicle when I spotted several does feeding on

This record-book Coues whitetail fell to the author's rifle while filming a segment of "Bass Pro's Outdoor World" in Sonora, Mexico. The Coues white-tailed deer, one of the smallest deer in America, stands around 28 to 32 inches tall at the shoulder.

a slight incline, which made them visible in the otherwise dense brush. I stopped the vehicle to glass them, hoping a buck might be nearby. That's when I spotted him, or rather a profile of his head and antlers as he stared at the does. There was no doubt that his tines were tall and "thick," and while I dearly love big 8-point bucks, at that moment I was thinking of the typical 12-pointer I had seen and passed up the year before in hopes that he might be even bigger this year. Still, I kept an eye on him as he watched the does.

To make a long story short, the buck finally looked my way and then immediately turned, quartering away from me. I could scarcely believe how wide and tall his antlers were. I got excited — overly excited. After failing to pull my rifle out of the Jeep Wagoneer I was driving, I grabbed my .309 JDJ Thompson/Center Contender pistol and followed the buck for about 300 yards before I could get a clear shot at him. Then after resting the handgun in the fork of a mesquite tree and taking careful aim I squeezed the trigger.

The buck took two steps and fell to the ground. One of the bigger bucks I have ever taken was mine. I looked down at my watch. It was 11:58 a.m. Don't tell me middle of the day hunting isn't good. Since that time I've taken many other good deer during the noon hours when most all other hunters are back in camp.

South Texas and the region of Mexico just below the Rio Grande have produced many interesting whitetail hunts over the years, including several hunts for a buck I called "Tobe." I first saw Tobe while conducting a helicopter game survey. His antlers were about 26 or so inches wide and he had 10 long points and drop-tines, each about 8 inches long on either side. I hunted hard for him as did the others who hunted on the property. We hunted him hard the following year also, and the year after that. But none of us ever saw him during hunting season.

I had just about given up on Tobe, but for some reason felt drawn to make one more hunt around a remote water hole where I had first seen the deer years earlier. Just about noon I eased onto the tank embankment and looked in the low-growing brush behind it. A deer was quartering away. He moved like an old man, slowly as if hurting from arthritic pains. A quick glance at his antlers and I thought I saw something hanging from his main beam, then realized they were drop-tines. Up came my .270 and I settled the crosshairs on his last ribs so the bullet would quarter toward the opposite shoulder.

At the shot, the buck stumbled and went down. Hurriedly I walked the 150 or so yards to where he lay. He was somewhat emaciated, his coat lacked the luster of a younger buck, but his antlers were extraordinary. He had 10 typical points with three drop-tines on his right main beam. I counted his points and came up with a total of 18. When the excitement started waning just a bit, I opened his mouth to age him. That was when I realized that he was truly an old deer, with teeth worn down to the roots. Later I had one of his teeth aged in the lab. According to the technician, the buck was 13 years old when I took him. Because of his antler style, where he lived, and his advanced age, there was then and even now no doubt the buck was "Tobe."

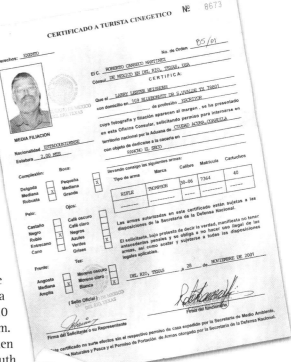

Times are changing in South Texas, some are good and some, well, it will remain to be seen the worth of some of the changes. But one thing is certain, deer quality continues to increase every year.

CHAPTER 4

A MORE NORTHERLY CALLING

have long been fascinated by what we Texans call "blue northers," fast approaching cold fronts, complete with dark threatening clouds, that bring with them cold and inclement weather. As a child I wondered where they had come from, and what they had seen while passing quickly over the lands to the north. Perhaps it was a bit of that "needing to know" that spurred on my first travels to the north. But more likely it was the lure of big whitetails that caused me to journey to the land of tall woods, vast crop fields, and winter snow.

Northern deer by their very nature are bigger bodied than the southern deer. It's a law of nature with most species that in order to survive in colder climates, bodies have to be bigger than the bodies of animals residing in warmer climates. The same holds true for whitetails. Bigger bodies also mean a larger and more massive bone structure and the larger a whitetail's skeletal system, the greater his opportunity to develop and produce larger and more massive antlers.

During the late 1970s I had read about the exploits of various whitetail hunters in Canada. I had also talked to a few enterprising hunters from Texas who had traveled up north to hunt deer, especially to the province of Alberta. The word was starting to get out that good, if rough, hunting was available in the Far North. Unfortunately, at that time, some of the other Canadian provinces restricted deer hunting to residents, except in a few limited areas.

My first trip to Canada was inspired by contact with Dick Idol. Dick, a regular hunter in South Texas, had been hunting the North Country for the past few years. Conversations with Dick, and the evidence provided by photos of some of the bucks he and others were finding, convinced me and three of my friends — Gary Machen, Murphy Ray, and Homer Saye — that we needed to make a trip up north. And we did, joined by Dick and another friend, Sid Lindsay.

The hunt took place near Carrott River, Saskatchewan, and primarily consisted of one big deer drive after another. Some drives produced deer, some elk, and two black bears, one of which I was able to take, and the other by Sid Lindsay. While we were not unaccustomed to shoot at running deer, we were not quite ready to shoot at 500 or more yards, the distance at which most of the shots presented themselves.

That trip was quite an introduction to hunting Canadian whitetails. But it hooked me on heading north. I'll tell you the results of this hunt a bit later in the chapter about missing B&C record-book bucks! Suffice it to say here the hunt was truly an experience. I have spent a fair amount of time hunting in Alberta and Saskatchewan and have seen some good deer, and occasionally a great deer, but for a multitude of reasons I never seemed to be at the right place at the right time. I was beginning to wonder if I was ever going to be able to take a Canadian whitetail. I needed an icebreaker, of sorts.

After returning home for several seasons with little more than my unpunched Canadian whitetail tag, I had the opportunity to travel to Quebec's Anticosti Island, located at the outlet of the Saint Lawrence River. I was hunting with Marlin's Tony Aeschlimann, accompanied by Jim Bequette, then editor of *Shooting Times*, and Bob Sarber from Petersen's Hunting. The trip proved a huge success. On the second morning out I shot a nice little 8-point buck, with a spread of about 12 inches. Later on that same hunt I shot a 5-point buck that was still in velvet with a new Marlin 12-gauge, bolt-action slug gun. I had finally broken the Canadian ice! If I had been anywhere else, quite frankly, I would not have considered shooting deer of this age or size, but our host had suggested shooting what bucks we could find, since the population that year was down a bit. Anticosti Island deer hunting was great fun,

OPPOSITE:
Larry Weishuhn dropped this extremely wide basic 8-pointer with a short drop-tine in Iowa on a hunt with Steve Shoop. The buck was taken within the final moments of a late muzzleloader season.

His mustache and beard covered with ice, Larry Weishuhn hunts the late Iowa muzzleloader season, one of the ideal times to encounter huge Midwestern whitetails.

all walking, still-hunting and spot and stalk. One of these days I would certainly like to return there.

The following fall I returned to Alberta to hunt with Ron Nemetchek. The hunt was, as all Canadian whitetail hunts are, an interesting one. It was characterized by cold weather, long hours of hunting, seeing few deer, and knowing that at any moment a record-book buck – possibly a new world's record – could appear. About halfway through the hunt I recalled Ron's words to the group of hunters he met at the airport when I flew into Edmonton for the hunt. "If you feel like you really need to kill a deer, Canada is not the place. Most of the time it takes at least three or four trips before you take a deer, especially one of any size. Yeah, you could get lucky the first time, but don't count on it." It was the same speech I had heard him make earlier that year at a hunting show to those who wanted to book a hunt with him. I felt fairly warned but still, somewhere, I knew there would be a sizable Canadian whitetail in my future.

I hunted hard, walking to my stand way before daylight and staying there until the evening when gray light faded to black. I saw only one doe, and that one just right after first light. The second morning hunt was nearly a repeat of the first day, but I did see a yearling 8-point buck. That same morning, one of my hunting partners, who also booked hunts for Ron, killed a massive 8-point buck, not far from where I hunted. Over supper that night Ron suggested I try hunting a different area within my unit, after the morning's hunt. That change gave me the opportunity of sighting the biggest live whitetail buck I've ever seen, before or since.

My guide and I were driving along an extremely busy highway when I spotted movement in the tall grass about 150 yards off the road. It looked like a doe carrying her tail at half-mast, almost always as a sign of being in estrus or approaching it. I commented to the guide about seeing the doe. He suggested we turn around and see if there might be a buck following her. It took some doing, but we finally got turned around and drove back to where I had seen the little doe.

She was still there when we stopped the vehicle. As soon as we did, a buck stood up and started toward the doe. The sight of that buck took my breath away. I had seen some truly nice deer in Texas, and I had seen many of the best and highest scoring whitetail racks taken in North America. I immediately knew I was looking at one of the biggest whitetails in the world, one that would easily net close to if not exceed 200 Boone & Crockett points. His mass was impressive and I seriously doubt his smallest circumference would have measured less than 5 inches. All of his tines were thick and long, the shortest, his brow, was easily 8 or more inches. His other tines were easily double the length of his ears including his front tines! When he turned to look at us his inside spread was easily 4 or 5 inches beyond his ears on either side. His main beams I am certain were very close to 30 inches. Years later I would take a buck in Iowa that had 30-inch main beams and this buck's beams appeared longer.

For about 30 seconds I got a very good look at the buck to evaluate his rack, but the one look I dearly wanted was viewing at him on the ground after I had shot him. But it wasn't to be. While the monstrous 10-pointer was indeed in the unit for which I held a license, we did not have permission to hunt on this particular property. There was little we could do but watch. All too soon the little doe trotted into a dense creek bottom and the buck followed. To this very day I can close my eyes and still see those magnificent antlers. I've spent time looking at Milo Hansen's

This big-bodied 8-pointer was taken while hunting with Ron Nemetchek's North River Outfitters in Alberta, Canada. Alberta produces whitetails that can be huge of body with antlers to match.

world record. I've also held the Jordan head, the former world record, as well as the Breen and numerous other top-10 of the world's whitetails. But to me none of them equaled the buck I saw that midday in Alberta.

After several days of trying, I finally got permission to hunt the property where we had seen the big buck. I hunted it from daylight till dark for three days, my last three days of the hunt. On the last morning of the hunt, a little past legal shooting time, I spotted a buck in the gray darkness of the icy fog. He was tall and massive. I pointed him out to the guide. There was little doubt in my mind the buck would have easily surpassed the 165 B&C mark, and quite possibly 170, but he wasn't the big one. I looked hard and long at that buck, which would have given me plenty of time to shoot, but I didn't. Then, like a ghostly apparition, the buck disappeared into the mist.

I spent the rest of the day hunting that property; then in the waning moments of the hunt, I spotted two bucks fighting and watched as they battled their way across an alfalfa field. One buck was a good 10 points, the other a much bigger bodied 8-pointer. I glanced at my watch — about five min-

The antlers on this typical Michigan whitetail rate in the B&C mid-180s class. This "northern" buck was taken on a preserve in Michigan.

utes of legal time remained. Very shortly my hunt would be over. I looked again at the big 8-pointer with my binoculars, then looked at him through my riflescope. I was convinced that the buck was at least six years old. Easing the safety off, I took a deep breath and then gently tugged at the trigger of the 7mm STW that I was field-testing. The congratulatory pounding on my back confirmed the buck was down. He certainly wasn't the big 10-pointer but he was indeed a worthy Canadian whitetail and one of which I was proud.

No one ever took the big buck we saw. I suspect he finally died at the jaws of a wolf or a pack of coyotes. I simply feel extremely fortunate to have seen such a deer, although I admit I would certainly rather look at him on my wall than in my dreams. That was the last year I hunted Canadian whitetails without a cameraman at my side.

The following year, cameraman and field producer Mike Pellegatti accompanied me to another hunt with Ron Nemetchek. I had met Mike the year before when he was filming a show for Tom Miranda. Tom and I had frequently worked on TV productions together, years before he became famous. That day I spent working with Mike filming segments for Tom's show started a longtime friendship. Mike and I have often worked on television shows together, especially ones we did later for "Bass Pro's Outdoor World" productions.

That particular season we were shooting a video segment for Hunter Specialties, and I hoped to take a good deer on camera. Before our arrival Ron had scouted an area near his headquarters and had found several bucks he thought would easily score 150 B&C points or better, excellent candidates for my hunt and the camera.

We hunted extremely hard in the areas where he had seen the bucks, and we saw a few does and a couple of small, yearling bucks. Although we didn't see a lot of deer, we did see a lot of wolf tracks, and frequently heard wolves howling. We kept hoping the wolves had not driven the deer out of the area, but we suspected they had.

Wolves, despite what some might lead you to believe, are efficient predators and quite capable of practically wiping out game herds. This was especially true in some areas where they had been reintroduced and overprotected in the early 2000s. Hopefully, in the long run, common-sense management techniques will replace the "natural"-predators-at-any-cost attitude often held by today's liberal and "dream world biologists."

After several days of seeing only wolf tracks, we headed to another area. Again it was coming down to the last day of the hunt. Personally, my dream whitetail hunt is to be on a week-long excursion and to take the buck of my dreams, or at least a mature buck, on the first morning. I get tickled when someone says to me: "As a writer I'll bet you love those last-moment successes, so you've got a lot to write about!" Quite to the contrary, my perfect hunt is to take an animal first day. That way I've got plenty of time to photograph and truly enjoy the rest of the hunt.

I had enjoyed this hunt quite a bit, even though it was coming down to the last day. That last morning my guide, Aaron Fredlund, cameraman Mike and I drove to an area where Aaron had gained permission for us to hunt in a place where he had seen

several really good bucks. As luck would have it, someone was already hunting on the property, albeit someone who did not have permission to do so. Rather than cause a commotion we headed to a different part of the acreage. No sooner than we had walked away, we heard a shot. Aaron suggested Mike and I continue on while he returned to see what had been taken.

Moments later he hailed us to come and look. In the field we had vacated less than five minutes earlier, because of our interloper, lay a buck with 15 total points, long tines and beams more massive than the buck's ear butts! Such is sometimes the luck of hunting Canada! We turned and headed in a different direction, and almost immediately spotted a sizable buck madly chasing does. Hurriedly Aaron, Mike and I devised a plan that, if it worked, would put us within less than 300 yards of the deer.

The stalk was a hurried one, trying to get quickly to the corner of the huge alfalfa field. We had almost made it to the corner when the first of the does suddenly appeared and started walking in front of us. Immediately I knelt down, set up my shooting sticks and rested my rifle in the crux of the crossed sticks. I glanced back at Mike to make certain he had the camera set up.

Six does filed past us. Then, there came the buck. Although not a monster, he was big of body, mature and had at least 9 points. I waited as he walked in front of us, then stopped, knowing Mike was getting everything on film. When the buck started to move, realizing something wasn't quite right, I pulled the trigger. The buck ran about 40 steps and fell. The film was made and I had taken a very nice buck which ended up scoring in the high 140s. There have been other trips with Ron Nemetchek, and hopefully there will be more in the future. I know somewhere in Ron's part of Alberta there roams a buck with thick, massive dark-stained antlers that has my name on him.

Over the years I have also hunted on several of the Indian reservations in Saskatchewan. Some of the trips have been pure pleasure while others have been a lot like hard work! All in all, none have gone as easily as we had hoped going into them.

A couple of the hunts were actually a bit on the scary side; once when my cameraman, John Tate, and I were shot at by locals, and another time when residents who did not care for the fact that the Indians had bought land where they hunted, suddenly put up no trespassing signs to deny them access. During the latter incident, they threatened to do bodily harm to the cameraman and me. While John is an extremely fine and otherwise even-tempered young man, he wanted to give them the opportunity to try! I convinced him the best thing to do was to simply smile at them and stay on our side of the fence.

That happened on a trip to a Saskatchewan Indian reservation with Bill Jordan of Realtree fame. Bill and I had hunted together in Texas, but that was my first trip with him to the North Country. We filmed that trip for the Realtree show and Monster Buck videos, and many viewers have seen me miss a buck running through the snow. It has always amazed me how many more people notice misses than they do good shots. On that particular occasion, I used all my cartridges shooting at that running buck and I still think that, had I been able to get my chapstick into the chamber, I would have killed him on that last shot.

Once again it all came down to the last moment on that hunt. During the waning moments, cameraman John Tate and I moved to a new area, and, with light fading fast, I shot a 165 B&C 10-pointer. For those who care about such things, yes, he was a bigger buck than the one I missed earlier in the hunt running across the snowy field. That night we boarded Bill's plane and headed south. He dropped me off at the Des Moines, Iowa, airport at first light. I rented a car and drove to Centerville to attend the Iowa Governor's Whitetail Hunt, to which I have been fortunate enough to have been invited several times. My hunting destination was Steve Shoop's hunting lodge. I had hunted several times with Steve in the past, both on properties he manages in Iowa and also in northern Missouri.

My first Iowa late-season muzzleloader hunt a few years earlier had netted me a huge buck, taken less than five minutes before sundown on the last day of the season. That old buck had main beams 30 inches in length, 10 total points (a typical 8-pointer with one double brow, and a 4-inch drop-tine on one side) and stretched the tape to 28 inches.

Steve Shoop and Larry Weishuhn pose with a 170+ gross typical whitetail taken by the author just before sundown on the opening day of the season. The hunt, part of the Iowa Governor's Whitetail Hunt, took place during a snowstorm on land managed by Shoop in southeastern Iowa.

A couple of years earlier while hunting with Steve in Missouri I got lucky on the first day of the hunt and at noon, using an in-line .50 caliber muzzleloader, shot a 24-inch outside, long main-beamed buck, that, had he not broken his left brow tine, would have net-scored above the 170 B&C minimum.

Hunting with Steve had been productive in the past and I felt confident I would do well there again. I had shipped my muzzleloader to Steve's camp before heading to Canada, but for some reason it was not in camp when I got there. Thankfully Jerry Martin, a longtime friend and captain of our Bass Pro RedHead Pro Hunting Team, had an extra gun in camp.

Over lunch Jerry told me how it was sighted-in and I

caught up on the goings-on of guys like Jim Zumbo (hunting editor for *Outdoor Life*), Jack Atcheson Sr. (of world hunting fame) and General Chuck Yeager, friends with whom I've shared several other hunting camps. Once I had caught up on the latest hunting stories, I headed to an area where I had hunted several times before.

This area was located on the edge of a field, where I have always seen deer when hunting with Steve. As he guided his pickup through falling snow en route to the stand, Steve told me of a buck he had seen recently. "He's got what looks like 12 points plus he has double brow tines, so he should be at least 14 or more points, and I suspect he'll gross over 170. I doubt he'll net book, but he's truly a good buck. The neighbor has been seeing him in the field each afternoon, right at sundown (end of legal shooting time), but with this storm having moved in and the snow, chances are he'll be out earlier." With that he dropped me off for the evening's vigil.

I crawled into the makeshift ground blind, raised my collar against the wind and snow and waited. About a half hour before sunset, several does and a couple of young bucks fed their way into the field. Occasionally the falling snow blocked them from view, even though they were less than 200 yards away. Time was slipping by seemingly all too quickly. I had been alternately watching the deer in the field, the woods behind me and to my left, where the trail led from the trees to the field. There was nothing in the woods or on the trail that I could see — I glanced at my watch. In about five minutes the hunt would be over for the day. Then for some reason I turned to look at the woods behind me to my right.

Through the falling snow I saw a deer walking slowly through the woods, some 150 or 50 yards away. A quick look through my Swarovski binoculars revealed it to be a massive antlered buck with what appeared to be lots of points. Hurriedly I raised the muzzleloader to my left shoulder, rested it on the log against which I was seated, found the buck in the scope and placed the crosshairs upon him. He was walking almost straight toward me.

The buck walked slowly, and I again glanced at my watch. Three minutes of legal shooting time remained. "Please turn just a little," I whispered as a prayer. The buck stopped and then apparently heard another deer walking up behind him. He turned for a better look back at his trail and in so doing gave me a broadside shot at his vitals. When he did, I pulled the trigger. Smoke and snowflakes screened my sight of the departing buck, yet I knew the hold had been good. I reloaded, put another cap on the nipple and started walking toward where the buck had stood. There, in the freshly fallen snow, I spotted several flecks of blood, then a few steps farther found bright, frothy blood, and then a broad trail of red mixed with snow. About 25 yards farther I found the buck. It was undoubtedly the buck Steve had told me about.

Thanks to the speed of modern travel and a considerable amount of luck, I had taken two whitetail bucks, one in Canada and one in the U.S.A., within a 24-hour period. A glance at the deer's antlers lead me to believe the buck might gross 170 B&C points. Later that night we gross-scored it at 172 and some change. Not only had I taken two deer in two nations in less than a day, I had taken two great deer, a 165 and a 172. I had trailed the hunter's moon north and in doing so had earned some most interesting and appreciated dividends!

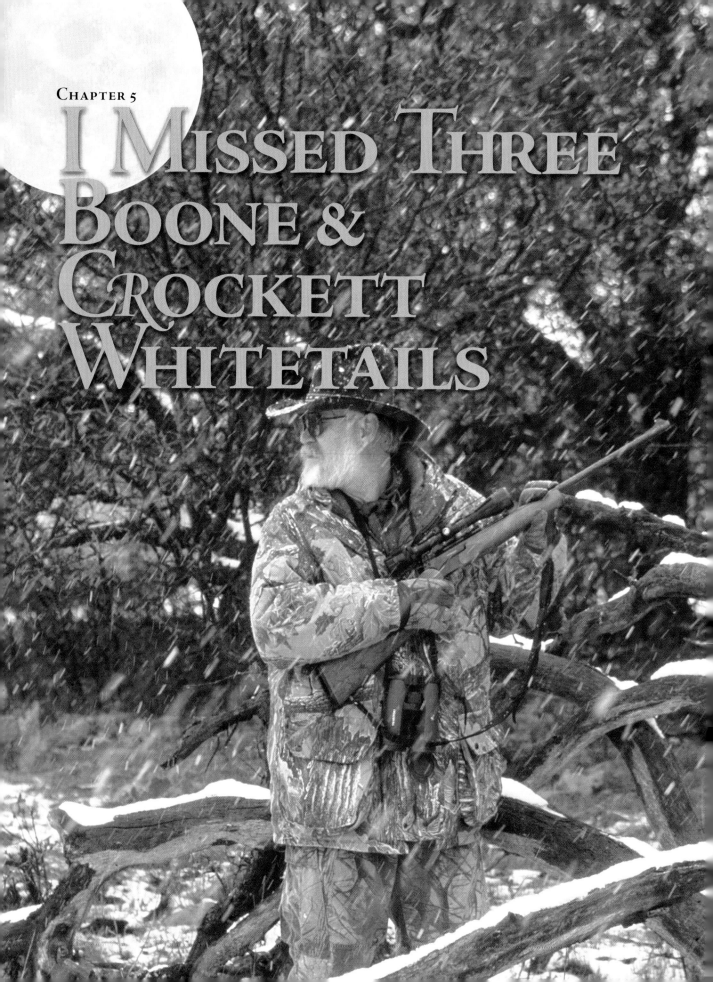

Chapter 5

I Missed Three Boone & Crockett Whitetails

Sometimes at night I wake in a cold sweat, worn out and somewhat distraught because of a reoccurring dream. In my nightmare – perhaps more aptly described as a "deermare" – the scene is the same. Three big whitetail bucks, two Canadian and one Mexican, keep walking by me and I shoot, and shoot, and shoot yet none of the three falls. I shoot until I'm all but out of ammunition and one last round remains. That's when I always wake up to the realization that I have indeed, thus far in my life, missed three Boone & Crockett whitetails. If someone were to analyze my dream with its one remaining cartridge, they might conclude that I'm hoping somewhere in my future there will be a fourth opportunity. Time will tell.

In previous chapters I've mentioned two of the three bucks I missed that were certainly B&C all-time record-book contenders and I hope that those encounters and missed shots taught me a few things. My first missed B&C opportunity happened on my first Saskatchewan trip, while hunting near the Carrott River in the eastern part of the province. The outfitter on that hunt was Kent Wolowsky and, as I've already mentioned, my hunting partners on that trip were Gary Machen, Murphy Ray, Homer Saye, Sid Lindsay and Dick Idol.

On the afternoon when I missed my chance, Dick was pursuing another big buck several miles away, but all the rest were present, and Gary Machen played heavily in the "deal," as you'll see. Joined by some local hunters, we decided to do a drive on a long, relatively narrow creek bottom. Gary, Murphy, Sid and I were instructed to walk to the edge of the creek bottom and act as standers, while Homer and about 10 locals started at the far end of the property.

My stand was supposed to be near a bulldozed crossing where I would be able to see the creek bottom and the other side down to a pasture road that paralleled the creek. A narrow spit of woods separated the road from a huge open field. Gary was set up a bit farther down the creek, but where he could cover the open field as well.

I had barely reached my stand when, in the distance, I could hear the drive begin. For some reason I happened to look down the road in the opposite direction from the drive and immediately spotted a huge deer running right down the road and toward me, about 500 yards away. I moved to a sapling next to the road to get a rest, and in doing so, I slightly changed angles so that I could not see the running deer. I stepped back out into the roadway and got down to get into a sitting position. Once again, because of the undulating terrain, I couldn't see the deer. So I stood up again.

The deer was still running right down the road and I had no choice but to try an offhand shot. Having walked down the same road, I knew there was a second crossing about 350 yards away. The banks of the creek were extremely steep-sided and about 30 or so feet straight down. I was convinced that the buck was headed toward the other crossing

OPPOSITE:
Standing in the branches of a fallen tree, Larry Weishuhn scans the snowy woods for his quarry. No matter how careful the preparation and skillful the hunter, the luck of the hunt always plays a role in determining the outcome.

The author's preference for hunting with a handgun is evident as he poses with a 300-pound whitetail taken with his 309 JDJ T/C Contender.

Doug Mauldin, one of the author's Canadian whitetail hunting compadres, took this huge basic 8-pointer in Alberta while hunting with Ron Nemetchek's North River Outfitters.

to get back into the dense creek bottom. There was nothing to do but stand on my two legs and take the best shot I could make shooting offhand.

Just as I pulled the trigger on the first shot, the buck jumped slightly to the left, just enough to sidestep the bullet. I bolted-in a fresh round and again put the crosshairs squarely in the center of the oncoming buck. I pulled the trigger again and the moment I did, he turned away from the creek bottom and ran into the narrow strip of woods. He was just coming out of the woods and I almost had the crosshairs an appropriate distance in front of the fast-running buck when I saw him nosedive into the ground at nearly the same moment I heard a shot from Gary Machen's .270. I let out a whoop, knowing he had cleanly taken the buck with one shot.

Gary and I met at the downed buck at the same time. I stuck out my hand to congratulate him and in typical Gary Machen fashion, he suggested I hold off with my congratulations until he was sure I had not hit the buck with one of my two shots. Even before we checked, however, I felt certain we would not find any bullet holes from the angle I had been shooting. Somehow neither of my shots had "felt" that good. There was indeed only one bullet hole in the deer and it was a broadside shot squarely in the animal's heart and lung area.

One close look at the buck's antlers and both Gary and I felt sure he would net book -- 10 long points, good mass, long main beams and about 23 or 24 inches of inside spread. We were right; later, after 60 days of drying, Gary had the head scored and it netted 172 and a couple of eights. Although I had missed my first Boone & Crockett whitetail, I could tell you his exact score, and the best thing about the buck was Gary had taken him. I could not have been anymore elated than if I had taken him myself. Had the roles been reversed, I know Gary would have felt the same way.

My second missed opportunity at a book whitetail occurred in the southern part of the North American continent, about 30 miles or so south of the Rio Grande, along the border with Mexico. My hunting partner this time was Ron Davidson. Ron has hunted throughout the world and the last time I visited with him, he had taken both a typical and a nontypical whitetail that would qualify for the Boone & Crockett record book should he ever decide to enter them. I've seen the typical and it easily nets in the high 180s. But at the time of the hunt, neither Ron nor I had hunted much other than whitetails. The ranch we hunted had a reputation of producing monster-size bucks. If the shed antlers we had found on the property were typical of the bucks living there, we were hunting some extremely good property.

Our hunt started a couple days after Christmas, a time when the rut is normally hot and heavy throughout northern Mexico. On the day we arrived, it started raining and the temperature hovered near the freezing mark. Camp was little more than a roofless old adobe house that did little more than provide a windbreak. Fortunately, for the entire time of the hunt, the cold, stout wind blew steadily out of the north. By putting our bedrolls tight against the northern wall, we were troubled only by the occasional rain.

The outfitter had suggested I leave my rifle on the Texas side of the border, since he could provide me with a rifle and there would be no need to tie up valuable hunting time trying to get a firearms permit. When I arrived at the ranch he handed me a Winchester Model 70 .264 Winchester Magnum, topped with a Leupold scope. He also handed me three cartridges. When I asked him if he had a range set up so I could see where the rifle was shooting, he told me not to worry as it was already sighted-in and besides, the only three .264 Winchester Magnum shells available in that part of Mexico were the ones I held in my hand. It was also time to go hunting.

According to the vaqueros, there was a tremendously long-tined 10-pointer that lived in the area where they had set up a tripod stand for me. The first afternoon, little showed but cold rain and two bobcats. That night I questioned the vaquero about the deer I was hunting. He assured me the buck would cross the fence-line sendero at 10 o'clock in the morning. When I asked him if he would cross there the next morning, his answer was *"quien sabe?"* His answer was the same when I asked if perhaps the buck might appear on day after that, his answer was the same followed by a shoulder shrug. After a few more questions I pinned him down. Sometime in the next week or so the buck would certainly cross less than 200 yards from where my tripod was positioned.

One thing I had learned by spending time in Mexico is that the local vaqueros know deer habits; they might not always know the difference between a mediocre buck and a true *muy grande* (even though they said they did), but they did know deer habits. So for the next six days I sat in the open tripod, from before first light until it was too dark to see. Each day it rained and the wind blew and it was COLD! Each night at camp I shivered in my wet sleeping bag, but with the hope that tomorrow morning would be the appointed, or perhaps anointed, 10 o'clock crossing time.

I'm a patient hunter, but after six, cold, wet and essentially "deerless" days (thus far I had seen only two does) even my patience was wearing a bit thin. It wasn't that hunting in that part of Mexico wasn't fun or entertaining. Throughout each day there were critters moving, but mostly javelina, bobcats (I saw an average of five bobcats per day) and coyotes in such numbers that I finally lost count.

The morning of the seventh day started much like the previous six: cold, wet and yet with the promise that today might be the day! About 9:45 that morning I was getting a bit antsy, wondering if indeed I should have put my trust in the vaquero and his recommendations of where to hunt. At almost straight up 10 a.m. I noticed movement about a hundred yards down the fence line. I did a double take when and extremely long-tined 10-pointer stepped into the sendero and stopped just before he got ready to crawl under the bottom wire of the 5-strand barbed wire fence. He hesitated just long enough for me to get the rifle to my shoulder, solidly rest the gun on the support of the tripod, center the crosshairs on his shoulder and pull the trigger.

I lost sight of the buck momentarily as the .264 Mag bucked up and back, but recovered just in time to see the buck cross under the fence and disappear into the wall of prickly pear and thorn bushes on the other side. There had been no time to get excited, barely enough to get a solid rest and pull the trigger. Yet I knew that the crosshairs had been firmly on his shoulder the moment I did pull the trigger, of that I had no doubt.

Slowly and deliberately I walked to the crossing. The deer's tracks were obvious in the wet sand. I immediately crawled under the fence and picked up his

A North Country guide uses his canoe to ferry a whitetail across a Canadian river. A canoe can be a valuable asset while hunting in remote northern areas.

fresh spoor, expecting to see blood and find the deer within only a few yards. Twenty-five steps and no blood, fifty steps and no blood a hundred steps and no blood. Surely the deer was laying only a few steps away. Better than a quarter of a mile farther I still had not found the deer or any signs of him having been hit. I stayed on the deer's trail and followed him for nearly a mile. At that point I finally conceded defeat, and headed back to camp.

There I set up a target at 50 yards, got a good solid rest and gently pulled the trigger. Through the scope I could see where the bullet had hit the target, a full 14 to 15 inches above the bull's-eye where I had held. My suspicion was confirmed; I had shot way over the deer's back. I had learned a valuable lesson — never trust anyone when they tell you the rifle is properly sighted-in. Next time, even if there are only three shells in camp, I'll set up a target and shoot one shot to determine where it's hitting, and I will fire the second shell to make certain that my adjustments are accurate. I'll save the third and final shot for the hunt.

The following spring I had occasion to be back in Mexico working on a ranch adjoining the one where I missed what I considered to be a "book" deer. Ranch hands found the buck's sheds; measured and allowing for a 15-inch inside spread, the buck would have netted 172, and he was at least 2 or 3 inches wider. So it goes!

I missed my third book deer in Alberta during my second hunt in the province. It happened one morning when we were "cruising" – driving slowly in a vehicle from one side of the property to the other. I spotted the deer crossing the road and could immediately tell he was an extremely long-tined 10-pointer. His back tines appeared to be at least 14 inches long and the rest of his tines weren't much shorter. He disappeared into some brush and trees. I immediately abandoned the pickup and ran to where he had vanished and started cautiously following his trail, hoping I could catch up with him.

I did about 200 yards into the thicket. He stood looking at me, with only rack, eyes and ears visible above a pile of logs. He caught me in a position where there was little I could do but look. Any move and I felt certain the buck would turn and be gone forever. We stood staring at each other. He had 10 points with about a 26-inch outside spread, massive and thick points that looked to be about 13, 10 and 9 inches in length. His brows I estimated conservatively at 6 inches.

There was no doubt, with his mass, that he would score above the 170 B&C mark. Still there was little I could do but watch and stand absolutely still. Time stood frozen and it seemed that an eternity passed. Just at the point when I was about to say the heck with it and try to quickly shoulder my gun in the hope that the deer would give me a possible shot by jumping back up the incline behind him, I heard noise behind me. The deer raised his head even higher and stared at the racket. Just then I heard the guide say, "You see him?"

That changed things in a hurry. As the guide's voice broke the silence and ended the proverbial "Mexican" or more properly "Canadian standoff," the buck whirled and took off running up the incline. I tried to get on him and momentarily I thought I had a clear shot and pulled the trigger. I thought that I might have hit him, but it was one of those nearly impossible things. We followed the buck's track for about 300 yards where he had headed through the woods, but there was nary a sign of his being hit by my quick shot.

Such are life's "little" whitetail adventures. In baseball I guess it's three strikes and you're out but in trophy whitetail hunting, I hope that's not the case. Maybe one of these days there will be a fourth opportunity. If there is, I'll certainly know of several things not to do!

HUNTING THE WIDE ONE

Depending upon where you started hunting whitetails, you've likely got your own system to decide what constitutes a really big buck. Where I grew up in Texas, the number of points on a buck's rack was paramount, and anything you could hang a wedding ring on was considered a point! In other areas, such as the woods of the Northeast, it seemed that the gauge of size was how much a buck weighed. Little attention was given to his antlers. Over much of the whitetail's western range, little else mattered other than how wide his greatest outside spread was. For the purist, the only true measure of a whitetail was the buck's net Boone & Crockett or Pope and Young score.

Me, I am impressed with mass and tine length. That is not to say that I don't also want him to have lot of points, long main beams, and be fully mature with a big body. Actually I've come to understand that some bucks that are a bit over-the-hill may have the most interesting racks. For the longest time the antler characteristic that intrigued me least was width — between main beams or even greatest outside. Not to say that I did not occasionally pursue a buck with exceptional width. What is a wide deer? To me it's a buck that has an antler spread beyond 25 inches, and over the years I've seen a few such deer and even hunted a few.

The widest buck I ever saw was one I was convinced measured about 32 inches outside main beams. I watched the buck grow up on a ranch in South Texas and saw him for about six years, each October during the annual helicopter game survey. Not only did this buck have extremely widespread antlers, he also had long tines and good mass, as well as long main beams. For several years he was a basic 10-pointer with all points longer than 9 inches, save the brows which were only about 4 inches. Each year I photographed that buck during the game survey. Later we projected the image onto a wall, enlarging it to the scale of the local deer by matching ear length and eye-to-nose measurements (the way a taxidermist determines which mannequin should be used to build a shoulder mount). Satisfied that we had duplicated the exact size, we measured the antler spread outside main beam. One year it was 28 and a bit, the next year it was a shade over 30; at the widest the spread measured 32 inches.

I've written about this interesting deer on numerous occasions. About how every year the buck moved about 12 miles as a crow flies from where we spotted him during the game survey to right behind the hunting lodge, where every afternoon he fed on the corn that a local ranch hand fed his horses. All this occurred without the hunters ever knowing that they were often within less than 200 yards of the buck, especially when they came into the lodge during the middle of the day to grab a bite to eat. He stayed in the ranch hand's backyard throughout the hunting season. In late January he would move back to his late winter, spring and summer home north of the headquarters area. That buck had brains.

One year while hunting in Mexico I saw an extremely wide deer, but didn't realize how wide until it was too late. I was sitting in a blind on a cold, wet, blustery day. The wind was horrible and every once in a while I peeked over the top of the blind to survey my surroundings. Off in the distance I spotted a buck; he was walking and all I could see of him was his profile. That profile made him look rather mediocre, an 8-pointer with about 9- or so inch tines and beams that appeared almost spindly. As the buck walked along, I occasionally glanced at him as he skirted the brushy edge of an opening that curved around me. I was not particularly impressed with the deer, but I'd glance his way to see where he was, and to make certain that a bigger deer hadn't suddenly replaced him.

Just before he disappeared into the dense thorn bushes and cactus, he turned to look my way. I could scarcely believe my eyes. His main beams spread way past his erect and forward pointing ears. There was little doubt the buck was very close to 28 or 29 inches wide. Before I could get my gun up he was gone.

In an earlier chapter I described an ancient buck I shot in Iowa with a muzzle-loader. It wasn't until I had gotten him back to Steve Shoop's camp that we measured the buck's spread. I had shot him during the waning moments of legal shooting light and had to drag him a long way in thigh-deep snow. I knew he was big, monstrous to be exact, but I did not realize how wide he was until I got back to camp. Steve's dad said, "You shot the buck everyone in this part of the country called the mule deer buck, because he seemed too wide to be a whitetail." But a whitetail he was, with main beams of 31 and 30 inches in length and a greatest outside spread that now measures 27 inches.

With that wide buck under my belt I forgot about trying to take an extremely wide deer. That was until I hunted with Tim and Trudy Schmidt on their Double T Ranch near Mason, Texas. I was there to rattle up bucks and shoot a management buck for a "Bass Pro's Outdoor World" television show. Off in the distance, close to 800 or so yards away in one of the few areas on the ranch where you can see that far, I spotted a buck that was wide — real wide. Through my 10x Swarovski binoculars I quickly guessed him to be 30 inches or better. I watched him chase a doe into a thicket and, as he moved away from me with his ears held high and back, he looked like he should have been 40 inches wide!

That night, just before supper, I queried Tim about the buck knowing that in the past his hunters had taken bucks that stretched the tape to 27 inches. I also knew

Larry Weishuhn and landowner/manager Tim Schmidt with the "wide one," a nearly 29-inch-wide buck Larry finally took on Schmidt's Double T Ranch. The hunt was filmed for the inaugural episode of the author's "Hunting the World" television show.

that bucks with 24- to 25-inch spreads weren't uncommon on his property. "Know the buck you're talking about." he replied. "We've been trying to get a hunter on him all year long. He's probably about 7 or so years old and we'd like to take him, if only we could," said Tim slicing some homemade bread while waiting for the roast-size steaks to finish cooking over the mesquite coals. He continued, "I've only seen him a couple of times this year. He's impossible to predict." he hesitated and then continued, "If we don't get him this year, ya' wanna come back next year and try for him?" Did I! The plan was set. I'd return on the opening weekend of the following year to hunt the wide one!

The day before the opening of whitetail season I drove through torrential rains, crossing flooded roads to get to Tim's ranch. Throughout the Texas Hill Country roads were under water and bridges were being washed out. But, by golly! I made it to Tim's property, as did my cameraman. That fall, just before hunting season, I had committed to do my own television show on the Outdoor Channel. If things worked out right, the wide buck of the Double T would be the premier star.

It rained all evening and when it got dark, Tim and I retired to the living room of his home after he told me that he had captured the wide buck on video for about 10 brief seconds. Sure enough there on the TV screen was a buck that appeared to be 30 inches wide, if not wider. We reran the all-to- brief segment of the wide buck over and over again, carefully studying his antlers, point arrangement and overall configuration as we could. Tim wanted to imprint the buck in my mind, because he also recently seen a younger buck that looked very similar to the older buck and he did not want me shooting him by mistake. I agreed.

"We saw your 'wide buck' (I liked the sound of that!) in the front pasture, not too far from where you saw him. That was about two weeks ago. The boys and I have been doing some serious scouting and try as we might we've not seen him since. But, being the case, we've set up a box stand big enough for you and the cameraman in the area." Before I could respond, Tim continued, "To be honest with you, I don't think you'll ever see him. But why not hunt for him a couple of days and if you don't see him you can switch to another area. I know we can find you a shootable deer if we have to." Sounded like a good plan to me.

I woke up periodically during the night to the

sound of thunder and rain falling hard against the windowpane. We were up and dressed well before daylight but it was still raining. Over breakfast, Tim suggested he and his son J.B. drop us off and then park just beyond sight of where we were, just in case it started raining horribly hard, or another severe lightning storm looked like it was going to pass through the area. I liked the idea, especially since I owned the camera we were using and I didn't particularly like the idea of sitting in a metal blind, acting like a lightning rod!

Daylight came grudgingly, but no sooner had it gotten light enough to discern shapes, I saw a deer walking in the cactus and brush studded field in front of us. It had the body configuration of a buck, but it was too dark to see antlers. I nudged the cameraman and told him to keep an eye on the deer and start filming if it stayed around and he could get enough light. Clouds threatened more rain and off to the east, lightning was flashing. I wondered if we were indeed in the right area for the big buck; after all he had only been seen twice on this side of the ranch. I knew that some bucks live winter, summer and early fall in one area and then when the rutting urges hit them will sometimes travel over considerable distances.

Slowly the light, what little there was, came up and lo and behold when I again found the first deer I had spotted that morning; he was still feeding on the tender green winter forbs near where I had first spotted him. I could see him clearly now. When he picked up his head, I momentarily forgot to breathe, my heart stopped beating and . . . it was him, the wide one. There was no doubt about it. He looked well over 30 inches wide and when he turned to look at something he'd heard behind him, he looked even wider.

"Get on him!" I whispered almost too loudly to the cameraman. "I am, but it's way too dark to get good footage!" came the reply I was dreading to hear. For a moment I considered shooting him anyway. But knew that wouldn't work. Slowly light conditions started improving, during which time great empires rose and fell and millenniums passed. I watched the buck. Prayers were being answered, not only had we found the elusive buck I had dreamed about almost daily for a year, but he was still here. I prayed he would stay until we got some footage and the cameraman said, "OK, take him!"

The buck continued feeding on the tender shoots, and a couple of does appeared and started walking toward the buck. He moved toward them. Thankfully, they were in low, scattered brush and cactus and about 40 or so yards from the nearest thickets. I waited, my beard turning whiter with each heartbeat.

"I'm on him, got good footage, take him when you are ready," came the quiet whisper from the cameraman.

"Huh?" I said almost too loudly. I could not believe it. We finally had some footage and I could shoot. Just then one of the does sidled over to the buck. He smelled her and flehmed. When he did, the doe started trotting away; her tail held at half-mast. It was now or never. The T/C Encore single-shot .30-06 rifle was trained on the deer's neck and shoulder. Ever so gently I pulled the trigger. At the shot the deer went down so quickly I scarcely saw it fall.

I kept one eye on the deer and the other on the spent case, which I removed and replaced with a fresh round. The deer never moved nor even quivered. He was dead.

"I don't care what you say, before we do any re-creates or cutaways, I'm going to go look at the buck. There's no doubt he's the widest whitetail I ever shot. I want to see him," I said to the cameraman in a stern fashion.

Quickly I crawled out of the blind and walked the 130 or so yards to where the wide buck lay, majestic even in death. He was absolutely stunning! After running my fingers over his horns and whispering a prayer of thanks, I headed back to the blind to do "TV stuff." I'll admit my knees were a bit wobbly as I walked back.

Hearing the shot, Tim and J.B. showed up and we did some "TV stuff" with them and the deer. Finally the recovery, cutaways and all the other things that are required when filming a television show were completed. Then we started shooting still photos for the many articles I would be writing about the buck. Little did the buck realize that in death he would become famous? But he did.

Later that afternoon we weighed the field-dressed deer. He weighed a little over 100 pounds. Other bucks on Tim's ranch generally field dress in the 140- and 150-pound range, and some even heavier. We checked the buck's teeth for age, and it appeared he was at least seven years old or probably older. The wide one had been born and was almost mature before Tim started his intensive management program and, for that reason, never quite put on the same skeletal mass as bucks born after the nutrition had drastically improved.

Because of the buck's smaller body, Tim and I were somewhat fooled by the spread of his antlers. Instead of being 30 inches wide as we suspected, he turned out to be exactly 29 inches wide. But who cares! I certainly don't; he's the widest buck I have ever taken, and probably will be the widest buck I will ever take. If you're into gross Boone & Crockett scores, and to me that's certainly a better measure of an animal than the net score, he grossed a bit over 157 points. Quite a deer, no matter how you look at him. Me? To be honest I truly enjoy looking at him on my family room wall. That's where I think he looks best!

About two weeks after the end of the hunting season, Tim called. After exchanging "Howdies" and a couple of hunting tales he said, "You shot the wrong deer." But before I could answer, "Well really you shot the right deer, but it turned out to be the wrong one." He then went on to explain that a couple of days ago he had seen another wide deer, a much bigger bodied deer with extremely widespread antlers with 6 points on each main beam. He suspected that the buck could possibly be an offspring of my buck, or at least out of the same gene pool. Was I interested?

Said I, "Remember all those lies I told you over the years about not really caring about how wide a buck's antlers are . . ." I could see him grinning.

Chapter 7

Mule Deer in High Deserts and Even Higher Places

W e're looking for someone to hunt mule deer with us in West Texas; are you interested?" asked Ernie Davis as he was about to walk out the door of our Wildlife Disease Lab. Before I could question him about the cost of the hunt, he continued, "Pretty good-size place just north of Kent; our scouts over that way tell me there are some pretty good desert mule deer on the property. I know you've been wanting to hunt mule deer. This would be a good opportunity!"

"Count me in!" came a voice from somewhere within me, not taking into account there would be a lease fee and I was not sure whether or not I could afford it. I had recently graduated from Texas A&M University and was working on Texas' Wildlife Disease Project, for a monthly salary that paid about the same amount that I would receive many years later for writing one magazine article. A biologist's pay wasn't all that great back in 1970, and my wife and I now had a baby daughter to care for as well. "Errr . . . ah . . . how much?"

"Only fifty dollars; you can pay me ten or fifteen now and I'll send you a bill for the rest as we get closer to the date we have to pay the lease." came Ern's reply. I wrote a check for $10 and hoped dearly that my wife would not decide to buy a week's worth of groceries that day; otherwise we'd be overdrawn at the bank. Perhaps I could do some odd chores to cover the rest of the amount before it became due. By working weekends at some odd jobs, I was able to put together the remainder of the money without dipping further into the family account.

For years I had read tales about hunting mule deer and listened to the stories of those fortunate hunters who journeyed north or west to pursue mule deer, and I had long dreamed of being able to do so myself.

My father-in-law, E.V. Potter and his brothers, had hunted mule deer for years in the desert mountains of western Texas, especially around the Marfa area. Quite often they hunted property that had not previously been hunted for mule deer, other than perhaps by a ranch hand taking a deer whenever he had enough money to buy a handful of cartridges for his .22-rimfire or "thutty-thut-ty" saddle gun. Stories of a wild, untamed land fueled and fanned the flames of my interest.

At the time, not having what I considered a proper mule deer rifle, I borrowed my brother Glenn's Savage Model 99 chambered for the .300 Savage. Topped with a Weaver K-4 scope, the lever-action gun shot with reasonable accuracy and would make a good mule deer rifle.

The Friday after Thanksgiving, Gerry Grevstad, a student who worked for our Wildlife Disease Project, and someone who had gotten onto the lease with us, helped me load up my Volkswagon "beetle" with a couple of tarps, a Coleman stove and sufficient groceries to last for about four days, if necessary. Rather than take a tent or lean-to,

OPPOSITE:
The decline in mule deer population due to changes in livestock grazing practices and an increase in predator populations makes bucks with sizable antlers among the hardest trophies to find in North America.

The author took his first mule deer high atop a nearly barren, rocky hill just north of Kent, Texas. For the hunt he borrowed his brother Glenn's Model 99 .300 Savage.

The reward of a three-mile stalk, this West Texas mule deer was taken while hunting in western Texas with Wildlife Systems owner Greg Simons. The mule deer buck, probably the author's best in terms of score, has 11 points, with tall tines, and better than 6-inch bases.

The Chinati Mountains in the remotest part of Texas' Big Bend Country are among the most beautiful high desert mountains the author has ever seen. They are home to desert mule deer, a whitetail that resembles the Coues whitetail and also the Carmen Mountains whitetail, found only in the highest reaches.

we each elected to put a tarp on the ground and sleep in sleeping bags between them. We were tough back then!

First light came bright and sunny and other than my stalking an upturned cedar stump (which looked for all the world like a bedded mule deer buck), for the better part of the morning I saw only a couple of does at a great distance. At least, without any good binoculars, I thought they were mule deer does.

As noon approached, Gerry and I met at a canyon mouth that spilled into low and flat ground. I looked at a ridge that lay to the north. "Want the high country or the side hill?" I asked. "I'm beat from walking up and down mountains and canyons. I'll take the low road." spoke Gerry. With that I started trudging up the slope, hoping to get just below the rimrock which ran the length of about a half-mile-long ridge. About 20 or so yards below the rim I started paralleling it. I soon spotted fresh droppings and a couple of bushes that had been horned by bucks. Below lay a huge expanse of lowlands and flats, stretching for several miles before meeting the slope of another mountain range.

I walked slowly, looking behind and above as much as ahead and below.

Hopefully if Gerry spooked a deer it would go up, and conversely if I spooked one it would go down. About halfway across the ridge I walked into an area covered with lechuguilla, a low-growing succulent type of spiny plant that looks somewhat like the pineapple plant. Walking through these sharp-ended plants is not unlike trying to walk on a huge porcupine's back. Surprisingly, it is a plant favored by both mule deer and javelina, which were also abundant in the area.

About halfway through the lechuguilla patch and watching very carefully where I placed my feet, I heard rocks rolling above and slightly behind me. Forgetting about the inverted pincushion I was walking on, I turned and saw a mule deer headed farther uphill and toward the crest. Looking up at him I could see he had the typical double split of mule deer bucks. He looked good and if I didn't react quickly he'd be gone.

I slipped the rifle off of safety as the lever action came to my shoulder, found the buck in the scope, allowed the slight bit of angle for a quartering away shot and pulled the trigger. The deer stumbled but kept on walking very fast. I levered in a second round and fired a second round. This time the deer fell! I let out an Aggie yell.

About the time I reached the deer, slipping and sliding as I crawled uphill, I looked down below and saw Gerry headed my way. At the deer's side I said a small prayer of thanks, and then stood there simply staring at my buck, my first mule deer buck. I ran my fingers repeatedly over his antlers and counted his points. He had 9 points, lacking the split of his back tine on one side; good brow tines and about a 23- or 24-inch spread. A pretty darn good deer!

I was practically beside myself with joy. It took me the better part of the day to cape, quarter and pack the deer back to camp, but it was not a chore, merely a pleasure! Such was my introduction to hunting mule deer. I was hooked!

The next year we again paid $50 per person to hunt the ranch. My hunt was cut short. By the first morning of the hunt my neck was swelling, the lymph nodes in my groin and under my arms ached and hurt. I felt rotten and, to make matters worse, when I got to really feeling bad I was about 3 miles from camp. It took some doing but I finally walked back to camp and left everyone a note that I was feeling really bad and had decided to drive the 90 or so miles to Van Horn to see a doctor.

When the old country doctor called me into his office, he saw I was wearing a hunting knife, hunting boots, and a green plaid shirt. His first question was, "Been up here hunting mule deer young man?" I hurt and wasn't too interested in talking, so I just nodded an affirmative. He walked around me and looked at the swelling under my neck and shook his head, and spoke, "Well you're not hunting anymore this year. You've got the mumps!" You need to go directly home and stay in bed, don't pick up anything, don't do anything!"

I walked back out to the little Volkswagon I was driving at the time, crawled in and drove back to camp, this year a tent. Once back I very slowly tore down camp, loaded everything into the little vehi-

Larry packs out the head and cape of his desert mule deer taken while hunting with Greg Simons just north of Sanderson, Texas.

Having shed orange for the photo, Larry poses with a truly nice Colorado mule deer taken with his .309 JDJ Contender handgun. The hunt was set up by Richard Petrini and his Tri-State Outfitters.

Land managed by Tri-State Outfitters under Colorado's Ranching for Wildlife Program in the state's eastern plains produced this huge, 28-inch-wide mule deer buck.

cle, got in and drove the 15 or so hours it took to get back home. I got back just in time to drive to our family doctor's office. He confirmed I had mumps, could not believe I had done all that I had, without them "dropping." He sent me home to bed and called my wife before I got home to tell her to send me directly to bed and keep me there, not to let me do anything. Needless to say I recovered from the ordeal, and hopefully wise, but also thankful I wouldn't be catching the mumps again. At least that malady would not mess up another otherwise good hunt!

That was the last year I hunted that particular property. After the season closed, a group of bankers approached the rancher who had been charging us $50 a person and offered to pay him $1,200 per hunter. Needless to say we lost our West Texas mule deer lease. Times were changing!

About that time I moved to Abilene, Texas ,and started hunting with Roy Bamberg and Chuck Dalchau, both with the Texas Fisheries Division. Together we started hunting desert mule deer in the Southern Lincoln National Forest of New Mexico. Back then that forest was a popular place to hunt desert mule deer and we quickly learned how to hunt it and be successful. Most folks who hunted it back then seldom if ever got farther than about a quarter of a mile away from any kind of road. By crossing the near canyon, scaling the opposite ridge and dropping into the next canyon, we not only lost all the other hunters but started seeing a lot more deer.

A lot of things have changed since I started hunting mule deer including deer densities. Mule deer populations have been in decline for several years across North America. Two of the big reasons are changes in livestock practices and the great increase in predator populations. When many ranchers in the western regions grazed sheep, they had a negative, but seasonal, effect on the range. Ranchers provide access to water by placing water facilities across the rangeland; thus they also disperse deer and other game populations across a greater area. Then too, ranchers, knowing that coyotes, bobcats, cougars and bears ate sheep, controlled the number of larger predators on the range.

When livestock grazing practices changed, so did the nature of the range. Today, in many areas, predation from cougar, coyotes, bobcats, bears and now from introduced wolves have taken a huge toll on the mule deer population. As a result the mule deer has taken it on the chin, and while their

chins as a species may not be made of glass, it's a compound mightily close to it.

Along the way elk populations have dramatically increased, and as elk populations expanded, mule deer populations began to decrease. The bottom line is, there is only so much browse and quality food available. Elk are bigger and require more food and can reach higher in adverse snow and ice conditions – again mule deer suffer. Friend mule deer has a pretty tough row to hoe in many areas!

There are bright spots, however, on private lands throughout the mule deer's range where interested landowners and hunters are providing better habitat for the species. Food plots are being planted to help them through the rough days of winter and, in some areas, predator numbers are being reduced to at least give fawns and older animals the opportunity to live a little longer. I've hunted such operations in several western states, both in desert terrain and also a bit higher up into the mountains.

One such ranch is in western Texas where I hunted with Greg Simons, owner of Wildlife Systems – a company that not only does an excellent job of setting up management programs but

Richard Petrini's Tri-State Outfitters helped Larry find this 190-B&C class mule deer during the fall of 2001. The hunt was filmed for "Bass Pro's Outdoor World" television show.

The long distances encountered while hunting mule deer require good optics, such as this Swarovski spotting scope.

also responsibly hunts those properties. It was with Greg that I made one of my most interesting mule deer hunts, on a ranch just north of Sanderson, Texas. Joining me on the hunt was longtime hunting partner Ron Porter who when I first met him many years ago was a game warden for the New Mexico Department of Game and Fish.

Ron took a nicely wide 4 by 4 buck early in the hunt. Since Greg and I were hunting for something special, we passed up several very nice bucks, nice even if they had been in the northern climes of the mule deer range.

Toward the tail end of the hunt, Greg and I set up spotting scopes and searched the distant horizon. At the end of a long, wide draw, better than a mile and half away, we spotted what looked like an extraordinarily high and massive buck. Thus the stalk began. For the next two hours we walked or crawled on our knees and belly past does and fawns, young bucks, the biggest and possibly the oldest fork-horn mule deer I've ever seen, as well as a 25-inch 5 by 5 buck. The latter we crawled past on our belly at a distance of about 25 yards.

Finally we approached the area where last we had spotted the buck we were after. We knew we were close. Moving at a pace which would have made a snail think he was a racer, we eased from one bush to another, suspecting that the buck was either gone or had bedded down. We hoped it was the latter.

Only a couple of bushes remained before the taller grass and scattered shrub brush turned to tobosa grass prairie, scarcely tall enough to hide a grasshopper. That was when we spotted the buck. He was indeed laying down, broadside and looking at something out on the prairie. I slowly raised my rifle from a glorified prone position, pointed it in the direction of the bedded buck less than 10 steps away and pulled the trigger. The buck's head simply slumped to the ground. The stalk remains the most memorable one ever! Our initial mile-and-half-away buck had a total of 11 points, with tall tines, and better than 6-inch bases. He's the finest desert mule deer I've ever taken.

Another one of my more interesting hunts occurred a few years ago while hunting mule-eared deer in Colorado with Richard Petrini who owns and operates Tri-State Outfitters. Richard had invited me to hunt on some property set up under Colorado's Ranching for Wildlife Program, which, among other things, allows hunting during the mule deer rut.

The property where he set me up to hunt was the Bijou Spring Ranch, a well-managed chunk of excellent mule deer, whitetail, elk and even bighorn sheep habitat. Hunting a few days before Thanksgiving, the mule deer were getting a bit frisky. I spotted and passed up several really nice bucks that on any other hunt I would have taken.

Later in the hunt, on a late afternoon I spotted a couple of very promising bucks at the crest of a saddle. Before I could make a move they drifted through the saddle and over to the other side. I slowly made my way through the oak brush and up through the pines to the crest of the saddle. There I took several deep breaths before peaking over into the small valley that lay beyond and to the south.

It was truly a sight to behold. The first critter I saw was about a 340 B&C 6 by 6 bull elk, feeding on the left side of the slope of the valley. On the

other side stood another 6 by 6 bull and three cows. Satisfied I had not missed any other animals on the real estate, I slowly eased forward, getting a look at a bit more of the hidden valley. As I did, I spotted the racks of two sizable mule deer bucks. Both looked good, but one was good enough to warrant a better look.

I eased forward and in so doing exposed more of the deer. The buck, which fed about 10 steps behind the front one, appeared to be the bigger and older of the two. He had typical double mule deer forks, good mass with about a 27- or so inch spread. I liked the looks of the deer, not only of his antlers, but his dark forehead patch, dark cape and extremely white muzzle.

I set up my crossed shooting sticks, being careful to move very deliberately and not make any noise. Up came the rifle, the fore end resting in the crux of the sticks. Through the scope I put the crosshairs exactly where I wanted the bullet, a 140-grain Nosler Ballistic tip .280 Remington, to go. When the crosshairs stopped shaking I pulled the trigger. The buck fell at the shot and did not move.

Just then I heard something that sounded like a critter walking up behind me. Immediately I turned to determine the source of the sound. I could not believe my eyes! There, less than 20 yards away, stood a full-curl Rocky Mountain bighorn ram staring directly at me. I had seen Rocky Mountain bighorns before, but never quite so close. The old ram stood and stared for close to two minutes, then turned and walked away. It had been quite a day of hunting mule deer. I had seen several quality and mature bucks, a number of elk including the big 6 by 6 bulls, taken an extremely fine mule deer buck, and now had been almost within touching distance of a Rocky Mountain bighorn ram.

Life was good. That afternoon the hunter's moon had risen a little early and truly shined a special light upon me. I hope it will do the same in the future on mule deer.

Wall tents, folding chairs and a fire circle provide a home away from home for mule deer hunters in their camp near New Mexico's Gila Wilderness. A well-run base camp greatly increases the pleasure of an extended hunt.

CHAPTER 8

PRONGHORN
PURSUITS

I am almost embarrassed to tell you about my first pronghorn antelope shooting experience. But then again, it is a tale that at least a few who have chased the prince of the western prairies can probably relate. Actually it was a collecting trip rather than a hunting trip. I was sent as a wildlife disease biologist to try to determine what was causing excessive "natural" mortality on the expansive Rocker B Ranch a way west of San Angelo, Texas.

I spent several days on the ranch looking for dead critters from which to draw blood and tissue samples. But none could be found. So the next step was to collect several pronghorn, at least two fawns, two does and two bucks (preferably older animals who had been on the range for several years). At the time, I was shooting my father-in-law's Winchester Model 88 .243 Winchester with a 4x scope. The combination was an accurate, attractive, appropriate package back in those days for pronghorn.

We entered a pasture where carcasses had been found in the past several weeks and as luck would have it, the first two antelope we saw were two bucks, both showing signs of age and both showing quality horns. Since neither my companion nor I had ever shot a pronghorn, I graciously suggested he shoot the one on the left then, as soon as he fired, I'd shoot the one on the right. Sounded easy enough! We were able to stalk to within about 200 or so yards of the two old bucks, which were standing under the scant shade of a mesquite. From a sitting position my companion shot at his buck. Before I could pull my trigger, however, the buck I was to shoot took off running.

PREVIOUS PAGES:
Backed by two observers, his rifle steadied on collapsible shooting sticks, Larry Weishuhn takes aim at a distant pronghorn antelope. The ability to make successful long-range shots is an important asset in the hunt for these wary, sharp-eyed range dwellers.

The author took this pronghorn at long range.

When judging a sizeable pronghorn buck at long range, look at the length of prong that extends beyond the animal's upward pointed ear.

No problem. I'd been shooting running jackrabbits for years and my target seemed to be simply a bigger and "slightly" faster running "hare." I swung the little lever action ahead of the running antelope and pulled the trigger and watched in amazement as dust exploded about 10 feet behind my target. I quickly levered in a new round, held a bit farther ahead of the running antelope and again pulled the trigger, fully expecting to see the antelope tumble and hear the solid "whump" of a bullet hitting flesh. But instead I saw dust fly up about 15 feet behind the speeding antelope. I levered in a third round and squeezed off another shot, and then another. All the shooting simply caused the buck to run faster, but in a great arc around my shooting position some 250 to 300 yards away.

I quickly refilled the magazine and, in fairly rapid succession, managed to shoot the next four shots with equal "efficiency." When those were finished I repeated the procedure once more to a total of an even 12 shots, all of which fell somewhat behind my running target. Finally the old buck tired of the game he was playing and started running away. I followed on foot and over the next several minutes, I shot four more shots — all clean misses! By now I was up to 16 shots, all fired without causing the buck to lose as much as a hair, as far as I could tell.

I reached into my pocket and found two more rounds. I put both in the magazine and continued walking after the now "somewhat" distant pronghorn. Back then I prided myself on my shooting ability. Taking this pronghorn was beginning to become a personal quest, and if it meant stalking him into the ground or staying with him until he died of old age, so be it!

I followed the pronghorn for a couple of miles and sometimes it seemed he was that far away. I was finally able to cut the distance to about 500 or so yards. I had fired the Winchester 88 at targets many times at that range and had even killed some whitetails with it at that distance; thus I felt I knew the hold. I found a spot to sit down, wrapped up in the sling, and as the buck walked directly away, I fired. Miraculously I saw dust from the bullet right at his heels. The buck apparently felt the dust spray as well because he took off running, quartering slightly away. For a bit I thought of saving the last bullet either for when I finally walked down the pronghorn, or saving it for me when I simply got too tired to go on. It seemed a tossup of what I'd end up doing.

As I sat there watching the pronghorn run, I decided to heck with it. I brought the rifle to my shoulder, found the tiny antelope in the field of view, raised the rifle so the buck was totally out of view, then moved the scope slightly to the right giving the shot a tremendous amount of West Texas windage.

I pulled the trigger when the buck, which was already no more than a tiny speck, was no longer visible in the 4x scope's field of view. It seemed to take forever for the bullet to reach the target. There was a cloud of dust when the animal fell and had there not been, I would have scarcely known it had been hit. I looked around to see if anyone was watching and hoped there was someone to witness the fact that I had finally connected.

I took off my hat and hung it on a lone mesquite within five steps of where I had shot. I tied a red neckerchief there as well; then I started walking in a straight line toward where the antelope had fallen. I stopped about 900 rather long paces later, still about 20 or so paces shy of where the antelope lay. About that time too, one of the other biologists drove up, laughing and shaking his head he said, "If you wanted to shoot him that far away, why didn't you just back up to start with. Sure would have saved a lot of ammunition and time as well. I drove in a straight line from where I found your hat and bandana. The odometer says it's a bit over eight-tenths of a mile. Brought your necropsy gear for you."

After a long and exhausting stalk in northern New Mexico, Larry Weishuhn took one of his better pronghorns — both horns are over 15 inches in length. The buck was unofficially gross-scored at just over 82 B&C points.

I thanked him and immediately pulled blood samples, made blood smears, did various swabs and then started dissecting the animal. Outside of the tissue damage caused by the bullet, the only major health problems I could see in the antelope were large, yellow hard globules in the liver. Interestingly, of the animals we collected, the buck I finally managed to take was the only one that had any obvious problems. In the lab the buck was proclaimed to have "hard yellow liver" disease, apparently brought on by plant toxicities. The solution to the problem proved to be a change livestock grazing pressure and fortuitous rain! To be honest, after that first antelope the rest have seemed a whole lot easier.

I've been fortunate to have been able to hunt pronghorn antelope in Texas, New Mexico, Colorado and Wyoming. I've hunted them primarily with rifle and also with handguns, more precisely the Thompson/Center Contender and later Thompson/Center Encores. Hunting these sharp open-eyed range dwellers with a handgun has added greatly to the sport of hunting pronghorn. Spot and stalk is by far the finest way to hunt pronghorn by getting down with them on their own level, you quickly realize how fantastic their eyesight truly is.

Not all my pronghorn hunts have been successful but thanks to the excellent management of the species, pronghorn are plentiful. Generally,

if you procure a pronghorn antelope license and shoot a reasonably accurate gun that you are fairly proficient with, your chances are fairly close to 100 percent you're going to take home a pronghorn.

That said, I will tell you that I have gone home empty-handed from a couple of pronghorn camps, and it wasn't because I was too choosy either! Try as I might, when hunting public land in New Mexico, I could not locate a legal buck on the property where my permit allowed me to hunt. Sure, I saw pronghorn, but only on adjoining properties, which were off-limits to me. But that's the way things sometimes go.

The pronghorn antelope is truly a fascinating big game animal and one that is uniquely North American. I'm not going to bore you with too much detail, but you should know that the pronghorn is one of the true wildlife management success stories in North America. You should also know that the pronghorn is the only true horned animal with branched horns and that it sheds the outer sheath each year. I won't dwell on the fact that they can seemingly outrun a speeding bullet, as I have already illustrated to my chagrin.

What is truly wonderful about this species is they are beautifully marked animals with contrasting browns and whites, possessing dark cheek patches and muzzles with nearly ebony-colored horns. I also appreciate the fact that if you want to sleep in one morning and start hunting pronghorn around mid-morning, you certainly can. Because they inhabit wide-open spaces, you can generally find them throughout the day without too much problem.

Finding a good buck in terms of horn length, mass, and sizable prong might be a bit of an undertaking, however. The best heads come from those areas where there is ample year-round food, and the bucks have a chance to grow old. While I've been fortunate and have taken several nice pronghorns, I've only taken one that I consider good, and I'm still looking for a better one. In my office I presently have the mount of a buck I shot in eastern Colorado while hunting with Richard and Bridger Petrini. I shot the buck on a lightning-lit,

windblown, rainy afternoon on a part of the Bijou Springs Ranch, which had been added since my first hunt there years ago.

We were scouting for mule deer in an area that Richard, who was extremely familiar with that part of the ranch, had said was void of shootable pronghorns, other than one buck he had seen a few days earlier. We looked for that buck but didn't find him and decided to look for mule deer. We found a bunch of 16 mule deer bucks, all with 8 or more total point count racks, which would have stretched a tape from about 21 to probably a little better than 27 or so inches. Most were probably on the upper side of those estimates.

To be honest we were engrossed in looking at mule deer and we were getting some great mule deer film for both "Bass Pro's Outdoor World" television show (where, as a member of the RedHead Pro Hunting Team, I served as a co-host) and my own show at the time, "Hunting the World." At that time I hosted as well as directed, produced and pretty much everything else you have to do when you don't have the money to pay someone else to do those things for you.

My cameraman at the time was not really what I'd call a hunter, but I'll give him credit, he had a great set of eyes. It was he who pointed out a dis-

tant spot on the horizon and proclaimed it "a pretty good goat," trying to imitate Bridger. When we put the big Swarovski spotting scope on the critter we agreed that he was a good buck indeed.

The only reasonable approach would be a long one on foot and we'd have to dodge lightning most of the way. That's what convinced me to carry my .30-06 T/C Encore handgun rather than a rifle — less metal to attract lightning bolts. The stalk was indeed long and just about the time we got into a position where I could take about a 200-yard shot, he spooked and ran. I watched him through the variable handgun scope, getting smaller and smaller in the scope view.

When he stopped, I mentally estimated the distance at just on the long side of 400 yards. In the past I'd shot at targets out to about 500 yards with the same handgun and I knew where the bullet should strike at about 400. I then held a bit higher, holding above and into the wind, using the buck's head as a reference point. When all looked good I squeezed the trigger. The antelope fell on the spot.

As we got close I commented to Bridger, "That buck went down in a hurry, almost as if he had been pole-axed." No sooner than had the comment slipped out, I stopped, "Oh no . . . hope I didn't hit it in the head . . ." I thought aloud. That's indeed what had happened, my bullet had struck the buck just below the right eye but did no obvious damage to either the cape or horns. Up close the buck looked really good, massive, decently long prongs, and over 15 inches in length. Later, one of the other hunters back at camp gross scored him at just over 82 B&C points.

I've seen a few truly monstrous pronghorns over the years, and perhaps one of these days I'll get one like the buck I passed up several years ago in New Mexico, which was later shot by my hunting partner, Ron Porter. That old buck, with his laid-down-over-the-nose horns, was just shy of 19 inches long. Oh well, thankfully Ron had taken him so I can at least go see him every once in a while . . .

Former New Mexico Game & Fish game warden Ron Porter, one of the author's longtime hunting companions, poses with a monstrous New Mexico antelope. Both horns are over 19 inches in length.

CHAPTER 9

ELK FROM BC TO NM

onder if this is a sight similar to what some of the first mountain men saw when they came to this part of the country we now call northern Colorado?" I asked my hunting partner, John Pflueger, as we sat transfixed, staring at no less than 500 or more head of elk scattered across the juniper and sagebrush covered hillside. The afternoon was quiet with the exception of ducks quacking and splashing in the beaver dams below and the gentle sound of a slight northerly breeze blowing through the pines on our side of the canyon. Below us, beaver dams halted the flow of a minor creek and flooded the willows and I could see several of the industrious creatures swimming with freshly cut limbs in their mouths. The sight is one most folks likely would have described as "pristine."

John must have been drowned in thought, for he took a long time to answer. "Amazing animals the elk; interesting how you can hear them all the way over here across the valley as they mew and chirp to each other. I'd like to know what they're saying." He hesitated for a while, looking intently through his binoculars. Finally he asked, "You seen any big bulls in that bunch? All I've seen are spike and a couple of rag horns. With that many elk you'd think there'd be a big bull amongst them." I had indeed noticed there were not many bulls for such a large combination of herds, only a couple of bulls that had 3 or 4 points per side.

As the afternoon wore on, we moved a bit to look at other herds of elk. The same thing was quite noticeable; the herds were practically devoid of bulls, and certainly there were none of any size. Perhaps it was because the breeding season was past and perhaps the bulls had again formed into bachelor herds. It was also possible that heavy hunting pressure on the vast adjoining public lands had taken too

OPPOSITE:
Larry Weishuhn poses with an elk shot while hunting with Jay Verzuh in western Colorado.

The author found this ancient bull in the mountains west of Steamboat Springs, Colorado.

This big, 6 by 6 bull elk, or one even bigger, is the dream of most elk hunters. Thanks to the interest of hunters and conservationists and the efforts of the Rocky Mountain Elk Foundation, bull elk of this quality exist in healthy, self-sustaining populations.

many bulls as spikes before they could grow older and produce better antlers. As a biologist I strongly suspected the latter. As a hunter, however, I hoped for the former.

John and I were hunting with our mutual friend Richard Petrini several years ago before Colorado set up antler point restrictions. Back then all bulls with antlers were legal and most of them got shot as yearlings. Today, thanks to a progressive management program and help from the Colorado Division of Wildlife, that same ranch produces large numbers of extremely big bulls.

Back in the late 1970s at the spacious J Ranch, elk were everywhere, but the herds consisted mostly of cows and calves. Bulls of any size were tough to find, other than a huge velvet horn spike, which according to the rancher, had been seen on his property each fall for the last seven years. His "horns" were about 36 or so inches long and probably close to 16 inches at the base, and looked at a distance much more like the horns of a Texas longhorn than an elk. Although I lusted for him, he was off-limits because ranch policy required that for an elk to be legal, the bull had to have at least 4 points per side.

Late one afternoon I spotted a bull high atop one of the peaks and it looked like he had 6 points per side. This was right behind our camp, a sheepherder wagon I shared with John. I began the assault on the mountain but it beat me. I had only gone about a third of the way up before it got dark. That night I decided to get up extremely early the next morning and be on top of the mountain by first light.

And, so help me, I was at the top of the peak at first light looking down on the rest of the world, totally out of breath and dizzy. I was there, but unfortunately the bull elk wasn't! I glassed and glassed and finally spotted some elk about two-thirds of the way down the mountain. They were a long way away, but I thought I could see branched antlers on one of them.

Immediately I started down the slope toward where the elk fed in a small park. I was making good time when I tried to traverse a small shale slide. About halfway across I lost my footing. Down I went, sliding downhill fast, grabbing at anything I could to slow down and stop from "skittering" all the way to the bottom. About 40 yards from where my "trip" had started I hit a small grassy area and was able to dig my heels and the butt of my rifle into the ground to halt my descent. I sat there for a few minutes trying to determine if all my important parts were intact. They were, although, scratched, gouged and extremely tender to the touch!

Finally I gathered myself up as best I could and limped across what remained of the slide. Just as I reached the small oak bushes on the edge, I faintly heard the bugle of an elk. Obviously the bull I had seen earlier was still there. Suddenly all of my aches and pains were forgotten and I quickened my pace in the direction from whence I had heard the bugle. Continuing on I ran into a series of relatively open parks and short rocky ridges, ideal cover as I eased slowly forward.

Then there he was! As I watched, the bull walked into a small park-like opening and started to feed on the lush grass. My first thought was to shoot from where I was, but then reason prevailed. The bull did not know I was there and the area where he was feeding appeared to provide good grass. He would probably be there for a while. If I took my time I could probably cut the distance from well over 400 yards to about 200 or so.

Larry Weishuhn found this bull high atop a mountain overlooking the Muskwa River in northern British Columbia. He fell at close range to one shot from a .300 Remington Ultra Mag, one of the first elk taken with that cartridge.

Tom Vince takes the lead as he and the author pack out the Muskwa River basin bull.

The author dropped this 6 by 6 bull in southern Colorado, while hunting with Dick Ray on a hunt sponsored by Winchester Ammunition.

I carefully picked my way down the side of the mountain, taking advantage of the cover offered by bushes, rocks and trees. Up ahead, I spotted a rock outcropping that looked as if it had been designed by a hunter as an ideal shooting rest. If I could make it to that rock, the shot would be about 200 yards from literally a rock-solid rest.

Bending down to appear more like a four-legged animal, I moved forward. The bull kept on feeding, apparently totally unaware of my presence. I stopped a couple of times and glassed him with my binoculars to make certain he had not moved. I also wanted to count his points. The second time I looked I counted the points again, 4 on one side and 5 on the other. The points were fairly long, as was his main beam. I wondered if perhaps he might be an ancient bull whose horns were on the downhill slide. The bull kept feeding only occasionally looking up to check out smells and sounds that surrounded him.

Finally I reached the shooting rock. I settled my .270 Win rifle onto the rock, got into a shooting position, and peered through the scope at the bull elk which was now quartering toward me. Whether from excitement, altitude, or just plain ol' bull fever, I was shaking quite a bit. The crosshairs bounced all over the elk. I started talking to myself, explaining how this was just another shot, nothing to get overly excited about, to calm down! An inner voice shouted back, "This is a BULL ELK! If you kill it, it'll be your first BULL ELK! SHOOT BEFORE HE MOVES OR RUNS AWAY!"

Finally I settled down and so did the crosshairs, which settled just behind his shoulder since the bull had moved to a broadside position. When all looked in order, I pulled the trigger, momentarily lost the bull when the gun recoiled, with lightning speed bolted-in a fresh round and found my target once again, running in a very tight circle. Soon as the shoulder presented a shot, I again pulled the trigger, bolted- in a third fresh round and fired again when a shoulder presented itself. Later that night when telling my story to John and Richard, both of whom had heard me shoot, they accused me of having used another rifle, stating there was no way anyone could work a bolt-action rifle that quickly, get on target and shoot. They were wrong!

After my third shot the bull went down and I was at his side moments later. He was handsome, gorgeous, and oh so big compared to the 100-pound whitetails I'd shot for years in Texas. I was beside myself with joy. After settling down I shot numerous photos with my self-timer camera, and then realized I would have to gut my elk, and then pack it down to the bottom of the mountain, where hopefully the cowboys could get some horses to pack it out the rest of the way. I learned a lesson that day about the size of elk and just how much they weigh, especially old bulls big of body and on the downhill slide of antlers.

That first bull elk was truly exciting but so were some of the others that followed, such as the New Mexico bull I took at the tail end of a long hunt. It was the year Thompson/Center first introduced the handgun they would eventually call the Encore. I had enjoyed the privilege of using the prototype Encore, then unnamed and the only one of its kind in existence, on a bull moose in Maine, a bull Shiras moose in Colorado and then on an elk hunt with Darryl Gilks in southern Colorado just above the New Mexico border.

For several days running, Darryl and I hunted a particular herd of elk, about 80 or so total, which was well populated with bulls, including one that would likely have scored in the 380s or better. Each day the routine had been the same. We crawled up the mountain while the elk headed into the pronghorn prairie country to the north. No matter what we did, we could not get ahead of the elk to set up an ambush as they tracked through one of several brush ravines which lead to the wide-open spaces. Routine? We'd crawl up the mountain then back down on the other side and hope we'd picked the right ravine. Each time we were wrong. Pure and simple, there was no knowing which one of the ravines they would take to feed onto the prairie. And, once there, they were perfectly safe, for there was no way to approach them where the cover was shorter than elk knee-length grass. Well after dark they would head back up the mountain, only to be gone again before first light. This went on for days.

As the end of that particular season approached, we were at wit's end as to

The elk, or wapiti, is the second largest member of the North American deer family. The massive antlers of a mature bull, such as this one, can weigh over 28 pounds.

what to do. Then things changed. Up until that time it had been unseasonably warm but one night a cold front blew in. With a northerly wind we could make a different approach to the herd. Way before first light we got in a pickup and drove around to the other side of the ranch and, just at daybreak, headed toward the top of a long relatively barren ridge that hid the valley beyond.

As we neared the top of the ridge I could smell the musky odor of bull elk. Just as we were fast approaching legal light and shooting time, the bulls in the valley beyond started bugling. Shivers like electrical bolts ran up and down my spine. I looked at Darryl. An evil smile came across his face and stayed there.

Using hand signals he motioned for us to ease up to the crest of the ridge. Taking advantage of the one nearby juniper bush, we crept to the top and looked into the valley beyond. It took a bit of doing, but I counted 72 head of elk, of which 21 were bulls bigger than rag horns. Several had 6 points per side. But try as I might I could not locate the monster. I had counted and glassed all the elk when a bull chased a cow from just below our sight. He had 6 good points per side and was wide. His head was held low as he chased the cow.

I glanced at Darryl, who nodded an affirmative. That was the signal I longed

A hunter takes aim at a bull elk in a mountain meadow. Stalking to get close to elk can be difficult, but it is easier when the bull's mind is preoccupied with cows.

for. Resting the .308 handgun on the juniper in front of me, I settled the crosshairs on the distant bull at about 125 yards. He was now quartering slightly away with his nose right on the cow's tail. I pulled the trigger and the bull dropped, simple as that! I could not believe it. The next thing I knew Darryl was pounding my back with congratulations. A few minutes later I stood beside my bull; the last day of the hunt had been good to me once again.

Another elk hunt that warms the cockles of my heart – but then all of them do – was a hunt in British Columbia, Canada, with Tom Vince from Muskwa/Prophet Outfitters, one of Kevin Ohmstead's outfits. Tom's father, Gary Vince, had once owned the area and Tom had returned for a special hunt, which was put together by Remington back when they were about to introduce their .300 Remington Ultra Mag. They had kindly invited me as well, and the hunt was to be filmed by Punky Rose for a couple of different television shows.

The Muskwa River area of British Columbia was one I had long read about and had heard tales of around many a campfire. Finally, I was going to be able to hunt there! After arriving and taking care of licenses and other paperwork, we were flown to a drop-camp about 25 or so miles from the base camp. Earlier, wranglers had trailed several horses into camp for us to use. They proved invaluable. When we settled into the Quonset hut camp, I noticed a huge, muddy grizzly paw print on one of the walls. Tom explained it this way, "Starting back when Dad owned this area we hunted a monstrous grizzly in this immediate area. We tried everything! But could never put a hunter on him. Each year, however, the old bear broke into this cabin and left a muddy paw print on the wall. And he's still here somewhere in the mountains, because that's a new print that wasn't there last year. I usually scrub the prints off of the wall – they have a way of scaring the clients," he finished with a wry smile.

With gear stowed and full of supper, sleep came slowly and I dreamed of big bull elk and of grizzlies that kept knocking at the cabin's door. We arose well before first light and while I washed the breakfast dishes, Tom saddled the horses. Back inside over a last cup of coffee he explained, "We're going to ride into a long canyon about three or so miles from here. Part of it burned about five or six years ago, and the elk browse is fantastic; it holds lots of elk and moose as well as sheep and goats. We'll spend the day and ride back to camp when it starts getting dark. Pack yourself a lunch. We can drink from the streams."

Moments later we were on horseback. I grew up around horses and owned horses and mules, but it had been a while since I had done any riding. After stopping to make some stirrup length adjustments, I was set. We followed a game trail created by elk, moose, and caribou which had followed the path of least resistance over eons of time. About two-thirds of the way in we passed a grizzly marking tree. Quite recently a bear had stood on his hind legs to leave a bite mark an easy 11 feet above the ground. The smell of grizzly evidently lingered in the area, because when I tried to rein my horse closer to the tree to investigate, he wanted no part of it.

When we broke through the timber and into the fertile valley of the large canyon where we planned to hunt we immediately started seeing moose sign, tracks and droppings. A bit farther up the valley we spotted a bull feeding on a tall grass flat. According to Tom the bull was about 50 inches wide and would have been a candidate to fill the moose license I carried with me, just in case. But the bull's palms were rather narrow.

INSET:
Larry takes aim with his T/C Encore handgun in .30-06 at a distant bull while hunting on Cotton Mesa Ranch in southeastern Colorado.

About 15 minutes later we spotted several elk on a slope high above us. Most were cows, but there was one dandy bull. We guided our horses into a small stand of spruce, dismounted and began glassing the feeding herd. The elk rut was under way and Tom suspected there might be more bulls around. At the top of the slope, where it broke into a high glacial valley, we could just see another bull.

The distant bull was considerably bigger in antler and body. He started bugling. Through our spotting scopes we could see him arch his neck, then open his mouth; it seemed like moments later we could hear his bugle. "That's the one we want!" said Tom, not taking his eye off of the bull. "I think the best thing to do is just stay right here and wait him out. There's a natural salt lick at the base of the slope he's on. He should come down sometime during the day."

The long wait was made a bit more bearable when I found a blueberry patch just behind where we hid ourselves in the

This 360-class bull elk was taken on Cotton Mesa Ranch in 2001, using a .30-06 T/C Encore handgun.

Larry Weishuhn steadies his Encore handgun on Stoney Point's Hunter Bipod, while Bridger Petrini of Tri-State Outfitters prepares to observe where the shot strikes the animal.

stand of dark timber. Lunchtime came and went, passing into early afternoon. Naps came and went, and finally the sun was starting to go behind the ridge. "He ain't coming down, we'll have to go get him. Saddle up, we'll ride as high up as we can then stalk him the rest of the way." came Tom's order.

The ride up was "interesting" to say the least. The old burn we traversed was steep and, despite all the switch-backing we did, didn't get us very high up the slope. Finally it got too steep for the horses and we staked them on lead ropes and took off on foot. About 200 yards up the slop, we were suddenly confronted by a rut crazed 5 by 5 bull elk. I doubt seriously that he had ever seen a human and he couldn't decide whether we were friend or foe. Behind him we could hear the bull we were after bugling. Finally, the young bull decided he'd rather be down slope of where we were. As soon as he walked past us, we continued our assault on the mountain.

Tired, weary and out of breath, we finally reached the same level as the bull elk. Tom alternately bugled and gave cow calls. The bull was close; we could hear him thrashing trees, and even hear him breathe before he bugled. We could hear his footsteps, but we could not see him, the saplings and vegetation were just too thick. It was also getting darker and soon we would be out of camera light. With hand motions Tom suggested we try to get closer and change our angle. To cover the sounds of our approach, Tom bugled and then thrashed the nearby bushes and trees with a stick to imitate the sounds of a bull coming in closer.

A few more steps and we could see the tops of his antlers — they were moving toward us. I positioned myself so I could shoot over Tom's right shoulder. I pointed to an opening and indicated with hand signals that if the bull appeared in it, I would shoot. The bull continued to advance and, as he did, I realized that the brush was taller than I had expected. I would only be able to make a neck shot as long as the bull carried his head high when he came through the opening.

Slowly the bull came. One more step and there would be a chance. When he stepped into the narrow opening I pulled the trigger. The bullet struck the bull just below the ear and literally picked him up and slammed him to the ground. Assured that the bull was down, I turned back to look at Punky. He was all smiles and I knew he had gotten it all on camera.

We approached the handsome 6 by 6 bull, hearty congratulations were passed, and we immediately gutted him, propped him open to cool. The cold night air would keep the meat until first light when we could return to pack him out. With field-dressing duties performed and a couple of sweaty shirts hung around to scare away any "predators," we headed back down the slope. By then it was dark, extremely dark. A hunter's moon was promised for later in the night, but it was still at least two hours away before it would rise. Finding the horses in total darkness was an ordeal as was getting them down the steep slope, but

I would not have traded anything for the experience.

I have long been fascinated with hunting elk with handguns, especially the Thompson/Center Contenders and later the Encore. In addition to the bull already described on the hunt with Darryl Gilks, there have been several others. Another one of my handgun bulls was taken while hunting with Ronnie West of West Outfitting, just across the border into New Mexico from where I shot the bull with Gilks.

The day before the season opened, we — Ronnie West, my cameraman Herman Brune and I — counted no less than 20 shootable bulls in the area where we planned to hunt the next morning. Surely we could get within shooting distance of at least one of those bulls. On the opening morning we were back in the same area well before daylight. The elk symphony was one of the finest I had ever heard during hunting season. Bulls bugled practically all around us.

Several sounded as if they were in the brushy valley that lay below the ridge that we were on, and one of those bulls sounded definitely like he was mature. Cautiously, we moved toward him, but in the process encountered a bachelor herd of six rag horn bulls. They were just below us and until they moved, there was little we could do but wait. Off in the distance we could hear at least 10 or more individual bulls bugling. I looked over at Ronnie — he was all smiles!

Finally the rag horns moved and we continued our quest for the bull, who had seldom stopped bugling, just around the next bend. We crawled on hands and knees to look around the corner. There he was, tending a cow, staying right with her going back and forth across a small opening. Hurriedly I set up my Stoney Point shooting sticks, rested my .30-06 Encore handgun on them and waited hopefully for the bull to reappear. I glanced back at Herman to make certain the camera was running and he was ready.

The cow burst across the opening and the bull right behind her. But before I could shoot, they were gone. But, I could still see the tips of his antlers as he moved around behind her. "If she comes across the opening again, I'll cow call as soon as the bull gets in the opening. Maybe I can stop him," whispered Ronnie.

I nodded an affirmative, then asked in a whisper, "Hundred and seventy-five yards?" Ronnie nodded. Just then the cow broke back into the opening and the bull started after her. The cow never broke stride from her fast walk, but the bull did, the moment Ronnie gave the cow call.

The crosshairs settled quickly on the elk, and, when all looked perfect, I pulled the trigger. Down went the elk! I heard Ronnie hoot and give what sounded like a sigh of a relief. I reloaded and waited for any sign of life, but the bull did not move. Later, at the bull's side, we confirmed he was indeed a 6 by 6 with massive beams, just as we had suspected.

Framed by massive antlers, Larry Weishuhn, Bridger Petrini and Richard Petrini pose with a three-legged 7 by 7 elk taken by the author in eastern Colorado while hunting with Tri-State Outfitters.

CHAPTER 10

WANTING BLOND BUT FINDING BLACK — BEAR THAT IS!

rack! Pop! Whap! It sounded like something or someone was walking through the Maine woods, headed in the direction of my bear stand, making as much noise as possible. At first I thought it might be a person "messing with me," trying to chase everything away from where I was hunting. Then, as it got closer, I thought it might be an extremely clumsy moose, because I had seen moose sign while walking to my baited stand. There had been moose tracks and droppings and there were rubs high up on trees where a bull had thrashed his antlers to rid himself of the pesky velvet that was peeling off of his now hardened antlers. Whatever the source, the sound was getting closer.

I was sitting on the ground watching a bear bait set up for me by Brent Bailey of Bear One Outfitters. Before heading into the woods Brent had told me of a monstrous bear track he had seen in the area. He suspected the bear might be visiting the bait. I wondered for a bit if perhaps the source of the sounds might be a bear breaking limbs and pouncing on logs to scare any other bears in the area away from his food source. Although I've hunted black bears for over 25 years, I have never heard a bear approach a bait station without making some kind of a racket.

Whatever was making the noise was coming closer. I spotted a patch of black moving in the bottom of the little draw headed right to the bait, a 5-gallon bucket tied to a tree, only about 15 steps from where I sat. There was no doubt it was a bear, and what little I could see of him was big.

I waited with my flintlock rifle rested on crossed shooting sticks. I didn't have a long wait. Into the narrow opening swaggered a black bear, the size of which I had never seen before. If he had had a hump I would have sworn I was looking at a black-colored Alaskan brown bear. The bucket was tied a bit above ground level and the bear's ample belly was above the 5-gallon can. In length he covered the entire opening. As he stared at the bucket, his head appeared even bigger by comparison.

As soon as I had seen him coming, I pulled back the cock of the flintlock and waited. Now, with the target within my sights, I centered the bead about two-thirds of the way down his shoulder and just behind. A hit there should cause the bullet to strike the heart and lungs and cause great damage to his vitals. It should also leave a blood trail that would be easily followed. The bear was either not aware of my presence or he did not care. He was certainly the king, lord and master of that part of Maine!

When I pulled the trigger, the flint hit the frizzen, throwing sparks into the pan — I simply heard a sizzling sound, no loud bang, no explosion of smoke as the flintlock sent forth its deadly bullet. Nothing! I kept the barrel pointed at the target, hoping it was just a hangfire. Nothing! The bear didn't move, but simply looked up my way with a most suspicious look on his face. He simply stood there not moving. I couldn't believe it! Hurriedly I reached for my priming powder, and started madly trying to reprime the pan. Just as I

OPPOSITE:
North American black bears, such as this 400-pound bruin, have been a passion of the author for many years.

Lester Weishuhn, the author's father, with two of his coonhounds turned bear dogs on their first black bear hunt near Ruidoso in southern New Mexico.

was about to finish, the bear turned and disappeared behind a screening of brush. For the rest of the evening, the bear stayed in the brush and trees, just beyond where I could see him. During the last hour of light he broke limbs, slapped trees, and occasionally woofed his displeasure at my disturbing his evening meal. The walk back to the road at dark was an uneasy one.

To this day, whenever I think of black bears I can still visualize the absolutely monstrous proportions of that bear. By the time of that hunt I had taken two bears, both of which weighed over 500 pounds, but this bear was considerably larger in both frame and bulk! I guess it simply was not meant to be. Back at camp the next morning I successfully fired the flintlock several times. Why it didn't fire earlier I will never know. Perhaps one of these days I'll encounter another bear of his immense size. If I do, I probably won't be hunting with a flintlock!

My fascination with bears started when I was young, sitting around a campfire listening to my great-granddad and his brother telling stories of their father hunting bears in the canebrakes and river bottoms of the Colorado River, near where I was born and reared. They told fabulous tales that had been told to them by their father about how the country used to be loaded with bear, but by the time they heard his stories, most of the bears were gone from that part of Texas. Still, on every trip into the woods behind our house I dreamed of encountering a bear. While hunting with my dad and his coonhounds I imagined that every one of the little bandit-eyed critters we treed were huge black bears.

It wasn't until I was out of college and working as a wildlife biologist that my dad, Lester, our cousin Crockett Leyendecker and I made our first black bear hunt with hounds. We hunted southern New Mexico near Ruidoso on property bordering the Mescalero Indian Reservation.

Remote water holes are ideal places to ambush bear during the fall season. Western bears come to water almost daily.

That first trip was a success and I was rewarded with my first black bear. I shot it as it came to a waterhole late on the first afternoon of the hunt. Although it only weighed about 100 pounds, I could not have been more pleased if it had weighed a thousand. I had taken my first bear, and that was all that mattered, size be darned! That same trip Crockett also shot a bear, as it ran in front of the hounds. Daddy never had the opportunity, but he was more interested in listening to the hounds than he was in shooting a bear.

During those early years hunting black bear, Crockett and I, and later Daddy and Crockett, journeyed north to Wisconsin. This was when you could still purchase bear licenses across the counter, long before you had to draw a kill tag. We had several excellent hunts and hound races along the banks of the Flambeau River and its tributaries. The first year we hunted there, Crockett killed a 300- or so pound sow and I passed up two smaller bears. I was hooked deeper than ever. Thus began a long journey that took me across North America in search of black bears.

I had always heard of the fabulous bear hunting on British Colulmbia's Vancouver Island and made arrangements for a hunt. It turned out to be an "interesting" one to say the least. Apparently, by that time someone thought I had gained some prominence in the outdoor field, because the antihunting groups caught wind of my hunt. When I arrived in Campbell River by plane, I was met by a screaming bunch of idiots, bent on disrupting my bear hunt. And to a great extent they did. They followed us everywhere we went.

There was little I could do but feel a bit amused by the entire situation, so I started talking to the "antis" — making pleasant conversation, if you will. In doing so I learned that most were not from Canada, and that the majority were being paid by an individual to cause me problems. Others were simply protestors who, if they had not been harassing me, would have been protesting someone or something else. In a way, they were somewhat like mercenaries, not committed to a cause, simply being paid to cause disruptions. The protests were not just "fluff," however, because while I was there the outfitter received numerous death threat calls, not only himself, but threats to kill his children. Serious stuff and seriously met, finally by law enforcement authorities.

Even with all the disruptions, screaming and hollering, I managed to see numerous bears, miss a couple for a variety of reasons (let's just call it bear fever), and finally managed to kill a sizable boar. That bear fell high on a hillside and no sooner than the guide and I had crawled up to the downed bear, two carloads of antihunter types pulled up beside our pickup. Thankfully, they assumed we were down in the creek bottom somewhere below the road. After about 30 minutes of searching for us, fortunately without looking up because we were in the wide open, doing our best to look like the natural vegetation, they got back in their vehicles.

As they drove up the road, which my guide knew dead-ended about three miles up the canyon, we got horribly busy, shot very few photos and then, in record time, skinned, quartered and packed the hide, skull and meat in one load. We got back to the pickup and were headed to town before they had a chance to turn around and find us. Interesting bear hunt — thankfully one with circumstances I have not had to repeat!

My second trip to Vancouver Island was much more pleasant; this one as part of a hunt for outdoor writers sponsored by Federal Cartridge. Jim Shockey was the outfitter and, as it worked out, my guide. Jim and I had a blast on that hunt. We'd known each other for several years and occasionally visited, but I had never hunted bear with him. Among others on the trip were Mike Larson with Federal Ammo, Ron Spomer, John Zent (editor of the NRA's *American Hunter*), John Barsness, and Ross Seyfried. Everyone in camp shot good bears, including several with skull measurements of over 20 inches. All were shot with 12-gauge shotgun slugs, field-testing a new round that Federal later introduced.

Shockey and I spotted "my" bear across a canyon. He was big and rangy look-

Larry Weishuhn displays the foot of a bear that squared in excess of 7 feet.

INSET:
Big bear tracks spell big bears. Finding tracks of this size, with a span of 5 inches, is cause for rejoicing.

Sam Ray and the author with a 500+ pound bear taken on Arizona's White Mountain Apache Reservation, using a T/C Encore 209 x 50 Mag muzzleloader. The bear proved to be the first animal taken with that particular combination.

ing, with jet-black hair typical of the bears in the area. We both knew he wasn't the biggest bear on the island, but he was darn sure respectable. The problem was that there was no way to get from where we were directly across to the canyon where he was. We had to walk all the way back to the mouth of the canyon and come up the other side.

We had barely reached the other side when we felt the slight breeze changing and blowing right up our backside. There was little we could do but hope to move at a faster pace to stay in front of our scent. The race was on! Back then I could still run a bit; this was before several helicopter crashes and resulting back surgery caused me to slow down. Jim and I took off at a trot, doing our best to be as quiet about it as possible.

As we neared where we had last seen the bear, we slowed to a walk. We were both certain the bear could not be more than 40 yards ahead of us. Hopefully, the bear would reappear before our scent reached him. Our pace slowed to near standstill and we anxiously looked for the bear. Suddenly there he was, less than 20 paces away, walking across an old logging road. In one easy motion I kneeled down, set up the Stoney Point shooting sticks, laid the Marlin bolt action slug shotgun on the rest, slid

the safety to fire, found the bear in the scope and pulled the trigger. All that took a whole lot less time to execute than to tell!

The 12-gauge slug hit the bear on the point of the shoulder and immediately he turned and disappeared into the thick, log-strewn canyon. I reloaded and Jim flipped the safety of his .300 Weatherby and ran to where the bear disappeared into the tangle. There was no sight of a bear anywhere, nor was there any sound of a bear thrashing through underbrush and limbs. We listened intently, but could hear nothing.

Five minutes passed and we decided to ease down into the thickets. Two paces down the steep slope we found a broad trail of blood. Ten paces farther we found a dead bear. A quick evaluation revealed that the bear had been dead from the time the slug had hit him, only his weight had carried him as far down the slope as he had gone.

The old boar was so black he had almost a blue tint about him. He was big as well, later squaring right at 7 feet with a skull that measured over 19 inches long. Of all the places I've hunted black bear, even though I've taken bigger bear in some other areas, nothing truly compares to the spot and stalk hunting on Vancouver.

Larry Weishuhn with an
enormous black bear
taken with a T/C,
50-caliber muzzleloader.

At the time of that hunt, Shockey was negotiating to acquire a hunting area in Saskatchewan. Two years later I had the opportunity to hunt in that area as well, on a TV show for "Bass Pro's Outdoor World." The fact that capped the deal was that Jim told me the area held several big, odd-colored bears — blonds, browns, cinnamons, and combinations thereof. Throughout my bear-hunting career I had wanted to take something other than a black-colored black bear.

Shortly after I arrived in company with cameraman/field producer Mike Pellegatti, I went to make certain that the .45-70 Marlin Guide Gun with which I was to hunt on that trip was still properly sighted-in. I was using Winchester's Partition Gold loads and the rifle performed accurately.

On the following morning, Mike and I set up a tree stand overlooking a series of beaver ponds. One tree was perfectly situated to cover the area. What intrigued me more than anything was the blond, brown, and grizzly colored hair I found on one of the beaver dams which, judging from the many tracks I discovered there, the bears used with great frequency. Not only were there a large number of tracks, they were also big!

On that first afternoon, we had a bear walk directly under our tree and put his feet up as if wanting to climb it. Thankfully, he didn't. He was an interesting bear and easily weighed in excess of 300 pounds, probably quite a bit more. He had what appeared to be a bald spot, just above his eyes and between his ears. I had noticed it when I first saw him because it appeared to be grayish in color. When he was right under us, I realized that he was not bald, but had a patch of lighter gray hair. Bald spots or even discolored hair on a bear's head are not that uncommon in the far reaches of the North. Sometimes during harsh winters, bears can suffer frostbite on their heads, which either discolors the hair growth or causes them to lose some hair.

The bear I've described to this point sounds mighty interesting, and believe me he was! Had I not been hunting in an area where there was a chance at a bear other than a black-colored one, I would certainly have shot it. I had found the hairs of much lighter colored bears and Clarence, my

The author and a guide paddle their canoe to a remote area in north-central Saskatchewan. The region is home to a large population of big, and often color-phase bears.

Outcome of the hunt — Larry Weishuhn and his Saskatchewan guide with a huge black bear taken with a .45-70 Government, Marlin lever action. This hunt was filmed for an episode of "Bass Pro's Shop's Outdoor World."

guide, had told tales of hunters seeing a huge blond, almost white-colored bear in the area the year before. Each thereafter we saw the bald bear, and occasionally a younger boar and sow, all black.

The hunt wore on, others in camp shot bear, including a fabulous light brown boar. One hunter shot a sizable bear as it charged him as he walked into the baited area. It was getting on to time to shoot a bear, or consider going home without material for a TV show. That was not a pleasant thought! Finally, one afternoon as it started getting late, I spotted a bear at about 175 yards coming our way. By comparing his height to the small trees that he passed, and his swaggering gait, I knew this was a bear — a real bear — undoubtedly the biggest I had seen on this trip, by far. Mike and I saw him at about the same time and was immediately on him with the camera, as if he could read my mind. Mike knew I had spent many years training myself to quickly spot game, evaluate it, estimate distance and execute the shot in a lot less time than it takes for you to read this statement.

Using a stick I had taken into the stand for the purpose of a rest, I settled the short-barreled .45-70 on the bear's shoulder, waited a few moments, and then immediately when it appeared to me the bear was going to start walking toward the brush, I pulled the trigger. At the shot, the bear whirled and started turning in fast circles and I fired again. With that, the bear turned and ran in the direction he had come from. I managed to get off a third shot just as he disappeared into the dark timber.

With fading light, Mike suggested we re-create the scene, shoot cutaways and then go look for the bear. We did so, but

in the process it started getting dark. With precious little light remaining I walked to where I had last seen the bear, found his tracks, and followed them into the dark timber. It was too dark to see his tracks in the woods and I backed out, confident he hadn't gone very far.

Several minutes later, Clarence came to pick us up with an ATV. I told him what happened and suggested we go look for the bear. He suggested we wait for better light and search for him in the morning. If he wasn't dead, a bear the size that we described might want to get "a bit western" if he wasn't dead when we found him. It's hard to argue with logic, especially good common-sense logic.

Back at camp we looked at the footage, especially of the shots. My first round had obviously hit the bear squarely through the vitals. My second shot appeared to have been a miss but my third shot had again struck the target. I felt much better after viewing the footage. I had a sleepless night, however, and I was ready to go look for my bear long before it was light enough to see.

I picked up his tracks where I had last seen them and immediately picked up a broad trail of blood. About 50 yards farther into the dark timber, I found the bear. He later squared in excess of 7 feet and had a skull that would exceed the B&C minimum, if I decided to register it for "the book." A great bear, but once again black as black can be.

Here, Jim Shockey and the author show off a mature boar that the latter took with a 12-gauge slug-gun using a Federal slug. The boar was part of Vancouver Island's tremendous black bear population.

My first truly big black bear was also the result of wanting to hunt where there were odd-colored bears. Shockey had invited me to come on a bear hunt with him on Vancouver Island but two days after that call came, I got a call from Sam and Dick Ray. Sam had just picked up part of the bear hunting rights on the White Mountain Apache Reservation in southern Arizona. A few years earlier, Jay Novacek, who played tight end for several years for the Dallas Cowboys, had hunted bear there.

A mutual friend told me that Jay had seen several odd-colored bears during his short hunt. When I questioned Sam about the color of the bears on the reservation he laughed just a little. "What color you looking for?" he asked. "We've got everything from nearly white bears to various shades of chocolate, brown, cinnamon, blond and even black-colored bears. Most of our bears are browns and shades of brown. Black-colored bears are rare." In so doing he already knew my reply because I had told both Dick and Sam that my dream bear was a big bear with a color something other than black. Sam then told me that there was a big blond bear that they

had seen regularly and that was the one we would hunt. I agreed!

When I got off the plane in Arizona, Dick Ray was waiting for me at the airport. As we drove to the reservation to pick up my bear permit and license, he started telling me about a big black bear he and Sam had seen. They guessed the bear would weigh over 500 pounds and easily square 7 feet or bigger. That's a big bear! Once in camp, with my gear stowed and my T/C 209 x 50 Mag Encore muzzleloader (then the only one in existence) loaded but un-primed, we headed toward where Sam had seen both the big black and the blond.

"I suspect if you see the big black, you'll shoot." said Sam as we parked the pickup and headed to a makeshift ground blind near where two bear trails crossed. On the way in, Sam showed me several bear tracks. Had the claws been longer, I would have sworn a grizzly made them. Sam just smiled.

The ground blind was between a water hole and a place where Sam had some bait set up. On the Mescalero Reservation it is, or at least was then, legal to bait bear. When we sat down it was about 3 o'clock. Sam had mentioned that he wasn't sure we would even see a bear, and if we didn't, we would bring in their well-trained hound pack the next morning to see if we could strike a fresh track. I wasn't particularly concerned about whether I would take a bear; it was simply a matter as to when I would take one.

About 30 minutes after we sat down, I heard the sound of footsteps on the dried leaves behind me. There was a slight breeze blowing directly toward where the sound was located and I felt sure that whatever was back there would spook. The footsteps, however, continued to get louder and were coming closer.

Ever so cautiously I turned to look behind me and saw a patch of black through the dense oak brush moving our way. If it continued in that direction, the black would likely cross a path to my immediate right. Slowly I moved my shooting sticks and set up my muzzleloader so I could shoot left-handed. This made a bit of noise but did not phase the black hulk coming toward us. Just then, the black crossed a tiny open spot. When it did, I could see the top of the bear's head. The first thing I noticed was that the ears seemed to be on the side of its head.

I pointed the gun at the opening where I thought the bear would appear at a distance of about 25 to 30 yards and concentrated on the spot because the bear had disappeared behind a thicket of oak leaves. I could feel the breeze still blowing from us directly toward the bear. Sam had mentioned that the big black bear they had seen in the area showed no fear of man. This one certainly didn't! Suddenly right in front of me, not 10 steps away, loomed a gargantuan black glob with beady intense eyes staring right into mine, and the evil I saw in those eyes sent a cold shiver up and down my spine. Almost the same instant our eyes met, the bear pinched his ears in a most aggressive manner and started popping his jaws. With that he picked up his left front foot and started toward me.

I had often wondered how I would react if charged by a dangerous animal. I quickly found out. I simply acted. Without any thought, I thumbed back the Encore's hammer, pointed the muzzle at the bear's oncoming chest and pulled the trigger! Smoke immediately engulfed the entire area around me; smoke so thick I lost sight of the bear. Out of instinct, I ducked my head to the right and turned away from what I knew was going to be a full-blown attack.

As I turned, I saw the barrel of Sam's .44 Mag, pointed in the direction of the bear. "That sonofabitch wasn't going to come any closer!" said Sam in a most determined manner. It was at that point I realized that the bear had turned and ran immediately after being hit by the 300-grain slug, from a distance of about 12 or so feet. Thankfully the bear had not been as mean as he thought he was going to be.

Sam laughed a bit when he saw that I had trouble reloading the muzzleloader. I sort of laughed at myself as well, albeit perhaps a bit of a nervous laugh. A few moments later we picked up the trail of "the old he bear" and almost immediately found blood, which turned into a broad blood trail. Seventy yards down the slight slope we found the bear. He was dead and was every bit as big as Sam and Dick had thought he might be, well over 500 pounds, squaring about 7 feet 10 inches and with a skull to match, easily above the 21-inch minimum should I ever decide to enter him for the B&C record book.

I was tickled, pleased, proud, excited and all the other adjectives that might be added to describe having taken a bear of such magnitude. But I still did not have "my" big odd-colored black bear. Thus the quest continued. Since that time I've continued to hunt throughout the black bear's range looking for that big odd-colored bear. I'll let you in on a little secret. I finally took my bear in New Mexico, hunting with Bridger and Richard Petrini, and then another such bear hunting with Tim Faries in British Columbia. One of these days when the hunter's moon is high above and the campfire is turning to embers, I'll tell you about those bears and the hunts that helped me realize a life long dream.

Color at last! Larry Weishuhn with an absolutely stunning cinnamon-colored black bear taken in New Mexico on a hound hunt with Bridger Petrini of Tri-State Outfitters. The gun used was a T/C Encore handgun in .450 Marlin.

CHAPTER 11

BROWN BEAR, MY TOUGHEST HUNT

I had been fascinated by bear for a long time and I could scarcely believe it when I was approached by Jerry Baker, an accountant in the town where I lived, with "Ever think of going on an Alaska brown bear hunt on the Peninsula?" Before I could respond he continued, "During the years I lived in Anchorage I got to know the Branham family really well, Chris, Dennis and I even met Bud. I think we might be able to arrange a hunt with them if you're interested."

Was I ever! I had first heard about Bud Branham when I read several articles in *Field & Stream* years ago by Warren Page, the publication's gun and hunting editor. More recently, I had taken every opportunity to stop by Jerry Baker's office, not only to visit with Jerry, but also to admire his Alaskan brown bear mount. The bear wasn't an absolute monster, but it darn sure wasn't a teddy bear either! Jerry had taken the bear a few years earlier and had been hunting there ever since, always in search of a 10-foot or bigger bear.

Jerry, needless to say, had my undivided attention and almost immediately after the invitation was issued, we started making plans for a spring Alaskan bear hunt. As we visited, he asked if I knew someone else who might want to go on the hunt with us. I knew just the person, Jay Novacek, tight end for the Dallas Cowboys. Jay and I had met sometime earlier and became friends, and with the bear hunt scheduled for before he would have to report for spring training, the timing was perfect. A quick call confirmed Jay would join us on the hunt.

I'm a serious student of handgun hunting, especially hunting with the Thompson/Center Contender, single shot and later the T/C Encore. As I planned my bear hunt I started thinking about which guns to take with me to Alaska. One would definitely be a T/C Contender chambered for the .45-70. I would also take my well-traveled Remington 700 .338 Win Mag as a backup rifle. Beyond those, I studied hard and long and finally hit upon the idea of taking a .454 Casull Freedom Arms revolver. That way if I got into a bear storm, I'd have 5 quick shots. The important things cared for, I madly started trying to get in shape.

In talks with Jerry and others who had hunted brown bear in Alaska's spring, I had been given the following advice: "Be in reasonable shape, but most of the hunting is going to be just below the snow line where the grass is green and lush. You shouldn't have to walk more than 500 feet above sea level, and chances are excellent you'll shoot a bear right on the edge of the beach." Now that sounded good to me. Little did I realize until the first full day of the hunt how erroneous that information would be!

The flight to Anchorage and the overnight there in the company of Dennis and Millie Branham felt like coming home, thanks to their gracious hospitality. The following morning, we loaded into one of the Branham's floatplanes for the ride into bear

PREVIOUS PAGES: Larry Weishuhn scans shoreside deadfall in search of Alaskan brown bear. The big bruins inhabit some of the most beautiful country in the world.

A base camp for brown bear hunters sits in the shadow of snow-covered peaks on the Alaska Peninsula. The camp provides comfortable lodging for weary bear hunters after hard days in the field.

camp, and a spectacular ride it was flying over high peaks and glaciers. As we neared camp we dropped considerably in altitude and flew low enough to see fresh bear tracks in the snow. We landed on a small body of water only a short distance from camp, which consisted of a couple of sleeping tents and a cook's tent.

In camp I met my guide, Joe Polanco. Joe normally runs his own guide service, but that particular week was open and he had agreed to serve as my guide. He proved to be a most interesting individual, who was as smitten with handgun hunting as I. That first day, having flown in and not being able to hunt, we worked around camp, settled in, made certain our guns were still properly sighted-in, and spent most of the afternoon and evening, glassing the surrounding countryside and exchanging hunting tales. Sleep that night on a full stomach, did not come easy. I kept awakening after dreaming that I had been charged by the "Monarch of Ursus Bay," recalling the tale of a bear charge I had read many years earlier.

On the first morning of the hunt I was introduced to alders and devil's club as we headed into the back country in search of bears. We found tracks in the bottoms and also spotted bear trails heading to higher country across what little snow remained. "Normally we still have quite a bit of snow this time of the year," stated Joe as he glassed a distant ridge, "but last winter there was very little snow and now the bear are scattered rather than usually hanging out just below the snow line. I suspect it's going to be a tough hunt!" We hunted hard and ranged far. Late

The author examines the tracks of a huge bear in the sand and gravel beside a small bay on the Alaska Peninsula. A big bear walked here. Even a mid-size brown bear print (inset) dwarfs the author's .454 Casull Freedom Arms revolver.

Hunter Jay Novacek and his guide use binoculars and a spotting scope to search distant hillsides for bear.

that afternoon, several miles from camp, we spotted our first bear, a relative youngster in the words of Joe. But to me it looked absolutely monstrous, even at the distance of about 600 yards.

On the following day we headed to an area across the little bay in front of camp. Immediately we found tracks of a good-size bear which lead inland. We followed a creek into the back country and just before noon spotted a bear so far away he was barely visible in our 20x spotting scope. Even so, Joe proclaimed him a huge bear. Around noon we settled on a rock overlooking the stream bottom and hillside behind us. I was being entertained by the antics of an otter when Joe nudged me and pointed to a bear high on the ridge behind us. Then there was another one. "Bet it's an old boar and a sow about to coming into heat, by the way they are both acting."

I marveled at the sight of the bears, the smaller of the two was almost a golden yellow. The bigger bear, probably the boar, appeared to be a grizzled brown. "What d'ya think?" I asked Joe. "I think he's probably about an 8-foot bear," he replied watching through his binoculars, "but he surely looks good. We can try him if you want to." "The stalk," he continued, "is going to be nearly straight up and it's

going to be tough to get within range." The rest of the day we tried and tried to get closer than about 700 yards of the bear, but we never could quite catch up to him. Had he been in the lower country, there might have been a chance but, having to crawl straight up – no way! Just before dark we headed back to our pickup point on water's edge.

The next morning we were back in the same area. But the bears had moved elsewhere. We spent the better part of the day glassing, looking at old bear sign and then glassing some more. On the following day we hunted yet another area and found bear sign but little in the way of actual bears. Jerry and Jay were experiencing much of the same, although Jay was able to stalk to within less than about 70 yards of a young boar, which he photographed.

The next day we moved to still another area, found huge bear tracks in the sand next to the beach, but no bear. That night, once our group rejoined in camp, Jerry and his guide Chris Branham reported seeing two bears a long way off in the distance and suggested we try that valley the next day.

Just past first light we stepped off of the little skiff that brought us to our jump-off point. Joe and I immediately started climbing up the steep sided hill. By then I was past the point of being sore and weary. What I really wanted was to simply lie in the sun for a day and heal up. But this would certainly not be a day for such nonsense! Chris and Jerry had been dropped off before us, and they too agreed to ascend to the top of the ridge and if they saw anything would direct us to it.

The crawl up the hill snaking through alders and fighting with devil's thorn was a pain-filled one. I was so tired when we reached the top I think even my eyelashes hurt! We sat down and ate a sandwich. About that time, I glassed Jerry and Chris; they were waving and then pointing toward the head of the wide and long valley that lay between us. I nudged Joe, and he focused his field glasses on Jerry and Chris as well. We looked at each other; suddenly all my aches and pains were forgotten. Obviously they were pointing at a bear at the head of the canyon. So away we went. Down into the depths on one side of the canyon and then up the other side, struggling through mud and ice, taking one step up and sliding back three. It seemed a losing proposition, but finally we reached the top of that ridge and glassed Jerry and Chris. Each time we put the glasses on them, they were pointing toward the head of the canyon still a long way away.

Joe and I walked, crawled, clawed, snaked, and wormed our way into and out of numerous side canyons, always headed toward where we knew there would be a bear. The day wore on, and we kept moving toward where we knew there had to be a bear. Finally, the afternoon sun was sliding downward and we were still headed in the direction of the bear, surely closer by now we hoped.

Seated on his bunk in a base camp wall tent, Jerry Baker checks his rifle to make certain there is a round in the magazine. Prowling bear make loaded firearms a necessity, even in camp. Baker helped organize the brown bear hunt.

Finally, we reached a point where we could see Jerry and Chris about a mile away, both lying down and snoozing in the warm sun. We were standing there totally spent, knowing we'd have to get back to water's edge somehow before dark. As I watched the napping hunters I saw Jerry stir and then sit up, pick up his binocs and look in our direction. We exchanged waves and, through the binocs, I could see him confer with Chris. Moments later they waved for us to come toward them. I wasn't too sure I had the strength left, but what other choice was there?

Slowly the realization set in that we had made a horrendous approach and in all likelihood there had never been a bear. We had just happened to glass Jerry and Chris each time they pointed something out to each other. At about that time, I happened to glass the snow-covered ridge below them and to their right. Out strode a bear and began feeding. Immediately after telling Joe about the bear, I started jumping up and down and waving wildly, hoping to get Jerry's or Chris' attention. Finally they looked our way and I pointed to their right. They got up and walked to the edge of the ridge and quickly spotted the bear. I alternately watched the bear and then Jerry who was getting into a shooting position. I knew the bear could not be more than about a hundred yards from where they were hidden on the ridge above it.

"Well, if I'm not going to shoot a bear myself, at least I'll get to see Jerry shoot one." I thought out loud. Just then I saw Jerry come out of shooting position and start waving to indicate that they wanted us to move in for a chance at the bear. For the moment, my body aches, cramps and pains were forgotten and Joe and I took off at a trot down the hillside. We guessed that we were a good 800 yards from the bear — first down the hill and then up. The kicker in the deal was a fast-running glacial stream at the bottom of the slope that we would have to cross before we started our ascent up the hillside.

I did OK until I got to the stream. Wading across a nearly waist-deep glacial stream is an ordeal anytime, but when you're dead tired and physically stiff and sore, it can be a totally different and quite dangerous matter. Despite my fears, I made it across. As we pressed on Joe encouraged me by saying, "Only 25 more yards." I guess I wasn't really paying too much attention because he used that ploy a good 25 or 30 more times. As I headed up the slope, there was nothing left in my body beyond pure determination; what strength there was had been washed away to the sea when I waded that stream.

Unbelievably the bear had continued feeding for the entire time, remaining near the area where I had first spotted it, drifting about 50 yards down the slope toward us. (Later I would learn why, because just behind her was a sheer drop-off of about a thousand feet. There was really nowhere else for her to go, and besides the grass there must have been exceedingly sweet.) "Twenty-five more yards," encouraged Joe. But I couldn't go another 25 yards. I looked at the bear feeding on the slope above us. It seemed to be no more than 75 or 80 yards, and I knew that even the bear was uphill and would surely charge downhill after I shot, I no longer cared. I had gone as far as I could physically and mentally. I looked around and found a rock jutting up a bit to form a solid rest. "I'm going to shoot from right here!" I must have said it with sufficient authority because I heard Joe say, "OK . . ."

The author negotiates a thicket of small alders along a stream-bed. Tangles of alders and devil's thorn create an almost impenetrable barrier for hunters, but brown bear have little problem moving in the low growth.

With that, I placed the 5-shot .454 Casull revolver on my daypack and laid my .338 Win Mag rifle right next to me in case it was needed. I took a few deep breaths, located the bear's shoulder in the scope and best as I could, held the crosshairs there as I cocked the hammer and slowly pulled on the trigger. At the shot, the bear, which had been standing broadside, fell and rolled down the hill one full turn and was again on its feet. I shot a second time and the bear fell in its tracks. It wasn't until later that I realized Jerry and Chris had also shot after I knocked the bear down the first time, fearing the bear would start rolling toward me. Later I learned both of my shots had struck the bear directly in and through his vitals. At the time, I was using an experimental Winchester handgun bullet and hoped to recover them. They both did considerable damage and exited. But that was later.

At that moment, I was watching the downed bear and mentally dancing a jig! I had taken an Alaskan brown bear, at the end of a harrowing 12-hour stalk — albeit much of the stalk pursuing an imaginary bear. Joe started up toward my downed bear while Jerry and Chris headed down to it. Me, I was bushed! To be honest, it took me nearly 30 minutes to reach the bear that had fallen only about 70 or so yards above me. As I headed up, all three of my companions were shouting congratulations down toward me.

By the time I finally reached the bear's side I was so worn out, I really wasn't thinking clearly. Normally, even with a black bear, I would have burned several rolls of film. Now I was content to simply look at the bear and rest. Thanks to Jerry, I did get several photos. To say I wasn't excited would have been an absolute lie, for inside I was jumping with joy and excitement. The bear turned out to be an ancient sow and, according to the information provided to me later, was so old she was beyond normal breeding age.

What really impressed me was her luxuriant hair coat. She was a grizzled brown and her shortest hair was probably 3 inches long. Even better, her coat was absolutely thick without any blemishes or rubbed areas. I was ecstatic with joy, even if at the moment I was too tired to show it.

After photos, what few we took, we skinned the bear, removed the skull and then started looking for a way off of the mountain. I won't bore you with details, but the descent to the sea below turned into a near death experience. Chris suggested we follow a slide down to the sea. He went first, followed by Joe. Jerry and I waited for them to call back to tell us it would be OK to follow. Finally we did anyway.

About halfway down, just below a small waterfall, Jerry crossed a narrow and very steep chute. As he reached the other side and I started across, rocks started falling and the entire slide started moving. Jerry stood on relatively solid ground opposite from where I stood and hollered loudly to warn Chris and Joe somewhere below.

I was committed to crossing the slide and there was no returning to where I had come from. The rocks under my feet were sliding down the hill, quickly gaining downhill momentum. I was running down the slope and, hopefully, across it as well. Although the chute and the area just below it seemed relatively narrow, it seemed to take me forever to run to the other side. Somehow I ended up below Jerry. I glanced to my right and saw him as I slid past. Below me I spotted an alder growing out of the side of the mountain. I dove at it, caught it and hung on. A few moments later the mountain below me quit moving. Jerry eased down to where I was hanging on. I stood up and we continued our descent.

Tomorrow there would time for rest, to recuperate and say many prayers of thanks. That night I fell asleep with my boots on. Tomorrow there would be time to celebrate. I survived my roughest and toughest hunt ever. I had taken my Alaskan brown bear and its luxurious and gorgeous hide was in camp. Following the hunter's moon had nearly done me in, but now life was good!

Larry Weishuhn and his guide Joe Polanco pose with Larry's hard-earned brown bear. Packing their trophy out through alder thicket and rockfall proved nearly as adventurous as the hunt.

Chapter 12

Moose, from Maine to North of Alaska's Artic Circle

There are no live moose in Texas and probably never have been outside of a zoo. So if I wanted to take a moose, there was no doubt I'd have to travel a bit to the north. I dearly wanted to hunt moose; nay I deeply wanted to shoot one of those mega-size deer, the largest of the deer species. So I began applying for moose permits in Colorado, Wyoming, Idaho, and Montana through George Taulman's United States Outfitters licensing service. The state of Maine allowed the naming of an alternate on license applications and through the gracious help of Thompson/Center Arms, particularly Ken French, my name was listed as an alternate on a whole lot of applications.

It was summer when I got a call from Thompson/Center that my name had been listed on one of the licenses drawn for a Maine moose hunt. They went on to explain that J. Wayne Fears' name had also been drawn as an alternate. Nothing could have pleased me more. Wayne was one of my favorite people and hunting partners. Beyond that, I never asked any of the details, simply started celebrating by going to the range with my T/C Contender.

A month passed and I received a letter from the Colorado game department stating I had been one of the fortunate few to draw a Shiras moose permit. I could not believe it. I'd been trying for years to draw moose permits in the lower 48 and suddenly I had two of them. I called both Maine and Colorado and, fortunately, neither of the opening dates conflicted. So it was back to the range once again with my Contenders.

At the time that I drew those permits I was serving as the hunting editor for *Handgunning* magazine (unfortunately, when the parent magazine company sold to

OPPOSITE:
Larry Weishuhn scans moose country — grassy meadows dotted with bogs and marshes, bounded by conifers and hardwoods — on his first Maine moose hunt.

Alert for danger, a bull moose cautiously leaves the shelter of a Maine forest. Mixed marsh and dense woodland can become significant barriers when hunters need to pack out their quarry.

Larry Weishuhn with his first moose. The bull was taken in Maine, using the prototype of the T/C Encore pistol, the first animal taken with the new gun. The bull's antlers feature two drop-tines.

INSET:
This big bull's antlers make a good rest for the handgun that took him, an Encore chambered for .308 Win.

Primedia, our handgun magazine was one of the fatalities). My goal had been to take as many of the North American big game species as possible with a handgun, realizing neither Mexico nor Canada allowed hunting with pistols.

About two weeks before heading toward Maine and my first moose hunt, Ken French called and told me not to bother bringing a gun when I headed north; he'd have one for me. I asked whether it was a handgun, rifle, or muzzleloader. "Can't tell you! You'll see it when you get here," was Ken's only answer.

The days passed slowly while I anticipated the first moose hunt. Finally, I boarded a plane in San Antonio and was delivered to the Bangor, Maine, airport where I met up with Wayne and Sherry Fears and then Ken and Pam French. Our ultimate destination was Ken and Pam's "Camp Quitchabitchin." On the drive to camp, Ken said Dennis Smith, a mutual friend of Wayne's and mine had already been in camp for several days and had been filming bull moose for his television show. I knew before heading to Maine that Dennis was going to film my hunt for his "Outdoors South" television show. I'd hunted with Dennis several times in the past and was looking forward to working with him.

Once situated in camp, Ken handed me a gun case and did the same to Wayne, but didn't say a word, other than T/C's R&D had finished the two guns only yesterday. I noticed mine was short and his was long. We opened the cases at about the same time. The handgun I held was sleek looking, reminiscent of the Contender, having a break-open action, but with more interesting lines and a bit bigger all the way around. I looked at the stamp on the barrel. It read ".308 Win." Wayne's gun had the same action as mine only with a rifle barrel and butt stock. It was also chambered for .308 Win.

We both took serious looks at the guns then asked Ken about them. He explained they were to be the newest addition to the T/C line and like the Contender would eventually have interchangeable barrels including shotgun and muzzleloader. "These are the only two in existence! And no we haven't even given them a name. Wanna go shoot 'em, see if they really do shoot?" asked Ken with a twinkle in his eye. At the range they did indeed shoot. From a solid rest I put three shots nearly in the same hole at 100 yards with the handgun. The rifle version shot practically as well. We were ready!

Moose season opened the next morning and Ken and Dennis had a bull picked out for me, one with double drop-tines. Dennis had filmed him a couple of times already. Before we headed toward where they had seen that bull, Ken and I wanted to check out an area where we had found a mammoth bull the year before while hunting black bear. He had many points per side, wide and long palms and probably would have taped 60 inches. If we couldn't find him we'd head in the direction of the drop-tine bull.

As we drove toward where we thought the monster bull lived we spotted some cows, and then immediately the drop-tine, which, according to Ken, was about five miles from where they had seen him a couple of days earlier. "What do you think?" asked Ken who saw my answer as I started loading up and grabbing extra rounds. We made a short stalk and set up at a distance of about 100 to 125 yards. My "not yet named" handgun was rock solid on the log I used as a rest. There was a problem — a cow was standing right in front of the bull.

Finally she moved, exposing his shoulder. I settled the crosshairs just behind his shoulder and pulled the trigger. We saw dust and hair fly when the bullet struck, but the bull did not react. I reloaded and as I did, the cow stepped right in front of the bull. It seemed like hours passed before she moved. The second she did, I shot. Again dust and hair flew from the exact spot I was aiming at. There was still little reaction and the bull now turned and started trotting away from us.

We moved toward him and the bull disappeared for a bit. Moments later he reappeared in a narrow opening and I shot him once again. This time he swayed and fell. I broke open the single-shot and reloaded again as we walked toward the spot where he was down. By the time we got there he was dead and, luck of all luck, he had fallen in the tracks of an old logging road. We would be able to drive right up to him! Standing next to the bull, I stood transfixed by his antlers and could hardly believe his size and bulk. His antlers were close to 50 inches wide and easily would have been wider had not a major tine been busted off on either side. And lo and behold he indeed did have drop-tines, one on the left and one on the right.

Moments later the entourage of 20 plus people that had been following us

The T/C Encore's designer Ken French and the author display the skull and rack of the first bull moose taken with the new handgun.

caught up. There were many congratulations! I was proud of my first moose, and a good one at that. That evening there was a fair amount of celebrating going on at Camp Quitchabitchin. Tomorrow we planned to look for a moose for Wayne. His came near the end of the hunt, also a 50-inch bull, which fell to one shot of his .308 T/C "hasn't been named yet gun." I persuaded Ken and the crew to allow me to take the new handgun to Colorado to hunt Shiras moose elk. He was reluctant to do so, but I promised to take good care of it, and return it as soon as I shot a moose and elk.

I flew back to Texas, drove by my home and picked up more clothes, and headed to Colorado to meet up with Jim and Madonna Zumbo. Jim had also drawn a Colorado Shiras moose permit and would be hunting in the unit adjoining mine. We had agreed to set up camp together, and Jim graciously stated he'd do the cook's duties. Although I dearly love cooking in hunting camps, Jim's culinary skill are legendary, and might I add rightfully so!

After setting up camp we started scouting for moose, driving the many roads in each of our respective units. We found two pretty good bulls in my area and then headed to Jim's. There we saw a bull that, in my opinion, was the finest moose I'd ever seen alive, dead, or mounted. The bull was wide with huge multipointed palms. As he quartered away from us I could count 18 on one side and I could not see the brow area. The other side had an equal amount of points.

Jim agreed it was by far the biggest and most impressive Shiras moose he or Madonna had ever seen, anywhere. Problem was, he was right behind an elk hunters' camp. When we set up our camp and scouted, we had seen very few people; what I didn't realize is that the opening of our once-in-a-lifetime-if-you-are-successful moose hunt started on the same day as did elk season, and this was one extremely popular place to hunt elk!

Opening morning the cameraman Realtree Outdoor had sent with me to film the hunt and I

With moose skulls and a triumphant banner, hunting companions Larry Weishuhn (center) and J. Wayne Fears (right) pose with firearms designer Ken French (left) after a successful hunt in Maine.

drove toward where Jim and I had seen the two bigger bulls in my unit. It was like driving through a city. Then when we got to the location where we had seen the bulls, there were camps set up in the same opening. Everywhere we went we saw people, lots of people. I could hardly believe it.

We hunted hard, and finally headed off on foot into the mountains hoping to escape the crowds and find moose that were doing the same. About two miles back into an area closed to vehicles, I spotted a bedded bull moose and made a careful stalk that eventually put me within about 60 yards. Only then did I get to fully see his rack. The bull, obviously a youngster, had probably been in a fight and broken off part of his rack. I considered shooting him for a while but then remembered the three miles I'd have to pack out of the hills and decided to keep on looking. Fortunately common sense set in before I pulled the trigger because it would have truly been a chore bringing out that moose, even in small pieces.

The next day we hunted in the morning and were riding on a forest road back toward camp, when a bull moose jumped onto the road in front of us, ran for about 300 yards only a few yards in front of our pickup, and then headed up the mountain. He wasn't of the antler quality I had hoped for, but pickings were pretty slim! We stopped the

Designer Ken French (left) and J. Wayne Fears admire this Maine moose, the first animal taken with the rifle version of the Encore handgun.

truck and walked up onto a plateau of cutover timber. I started glassing and about 150 yards away I spotted the same bull we had just seen. He was bedded down and looking the other way.

I loaded my .308 handgun and began my stalk, with the cameraman right behind me. We were able to get within about 75 yards before we ran out of stalking cover. There, I found a convenient stump and rested the handgun. The bull was lying down and obviously was in no hurry to get up. We waited, and waited, and waited, but he just lay there. Finally I told the cameraman I was going to shoot.

I picked a spot behind his shoulder, steadied the crosshairs and pulled the trigger. At the shot, the bull stood up and I reloaded and fired again and then again. At that point the bull turned and exposed his other side to me. I shot him twice more before he fell. Later, just as with the Maine bull, I learned the first shot was a killing shot. Sometimes moose just take a bit of convincing.

It didn't take me long to walk to the downed

Two weeks after taking his first moose, Larry Weishuhn killed this Colorado Shiras moose; once again using the then unnamed T/C Encore handgun.

moose. He had about a 35- or 36-inch spread, and a huge body. Considering the fiasco of having to compete with all the people on this once-in-a-lifetime hunt, I was extremely pleased with my bull. I knew among other things he would be excellent eating, and indeed he was. I shared the bounty with Zumbo, who, as it worked out, never saw a bull moose during the entire week we hunted. All Jim could find was people, people and more people.

Eventually I had to return the T/C handgun, which I introduced to the world in the pages of *Handgunning* and *Shooting Times* as the T/C Encore. It has become my all-time favorite handgun and rifle. By the time I hunted moose in Wyoming (thanks to drawing a permit), the Encore had been named.

My hunt for Wyoming moose in the Bighorn Mountains was with Toby Johnson, who was something of a legend among outfitters and worldwide hunters. Toby knew the mountains like an accountant knows his numbers. The hunt was fun but also tough and we hunted hard day after day but simply could not find any moose. There was plenty of sign but moose simply avoided us. Finally the Realtree cameraman, who had accompanied me throughout the hunt had to leave. Toby suggested I stay on at least a couple more days. I agreed; I'd invested too much time to give up now.

On the second to last day of the hunt, Toby and I picked up a track in fresh snow, this just after first light. Throughout the day we followed the tracks from the bottom of the canyon to the top of the ridge, then back down again and then back to the top of the ridge (above timberline) and then back down again. We knew he was a bull; you could see where his antlers knocked snow off of limbs as he walked. Apparently the bull was working scrapes and looking for cows. When it got too dark to follow the bull's tracks, we headed back to the pickup, miles away.

Before first light the next morning, Brant Hillman, Toby's chief guide, and I headed back to the area where we had stopped following the tracks. We drove as far as we could, then took the ATV to the edge of the wilderness area. There we started walking up the mountain on a backpacker trail. We walked just shy of a mile when I asked Brant, "Wouldn't it be great if a bull just walked across the trail right in front of us?" He laughed and commented he doubted that would ever happen.

Sometimes life is full of little surprises. Not 20 steps farther I spotted something dark up above us about a hundred yards away. At first I thought it might be a horse or cow, then remembered this was a wilderness area without any livestock. Just then I spotted antlers. A quick look and yes both were there. Before I could say anything, Brant was pointing as well.

A few steps ahead, a convenient forked tree provided an ideal handgun rest. My first shot from the .30-06 Encore struck the bull right behind the shoulder. He took a couple of steps and I hit him again with a second round almost in the same place. He stopped. My third shot hit him in the neck a few inches behind and below his ear. The bull fell to the ground. I was pleased to no end with my Wyoming, Shiras moose. I had hunted hard and long and, with the season fading fast, finally had taken my animal. After pictures, Brant and I worked together with the skinning, caping, quartering and packing. In almost record time we had the entire moose on the back of the ATV and were on our way home.

Alaskan moose are undoubtedly the biggest of the species, and as luck would have it, my toughest moose thus far. That's not to say, however, that the Wyoming moose hunt was an easy one. At a North American Hunting Club Jamboree I met with Henry Clark of Kobuk Guides and Outfitters. I had known Henry for a while, but had never hunted with him; but when he invited me to hunt moose and caribou with him on the northern slopes of Alaska's Brooks Range, I jumped at the chance, especially since Alaska allows hunting with handguns.

I arrived in Kotzebue, Alaska, tired but happy to be there. At the airport I met Henry. We stowed my gear, drove to town, purchased licenses and then headed back to the airport for the flight to camp. "Since you can't hunt today, wanna go look at some country with me, and maybe check on a camp or two?" invited Henry. That sounded like an excellent plan. For the next two hours Henry and I flew between his camps and also looked at a tremendous amount of game, caribou, moose and even a monstrous almost chocolate-colored grizzly. I should add a couple of the moose we saw, unfortunately too far away to be able to pack out all the meat, were absolute monsters, easily over 70 inches wide. We circled one of them a couple of times. Not only was he wide, but the palms of his antlers were extremely long and wide with many long points.

Finally we set down at camp, a series of tents next to a flowing river. The plan

This substantial Shiras moose was taken by the author in Wyoming using a .30–06 T/C Encore handgun, while hunting with Toby Johnson and guide Brant Hillman.

was to hunt around base camp a few days and then possibly head to a drop camp. But weather has a way of changing things in Alaska. The day I arrived in camp the sky was blue and nary a cloud was to be seen. That night it started raining, not your normal Alaskan kind of rain, but the kind of rain that pours and never quits. During the next few days my guide and Henry's partner in the outfitting business, Wayne Taylor, and I hunted hard and most wet. My agreement with Henry was to hunt until I shot a caribou and a moose or until the end of moose season, whichever came first.

Wayne and I had lots of fun hunting together, but the weather or something caused the caribou to quit moving and essentially shut the moose rut down to zero. Still we hunted. But the only moose we were seeing were the racks left in camp to be shipped later and the same was true for caribou. We did find one fairly fresh grizzly killed moose that made for some rather intense moments as we backed out of the thicket where the grizzly had it cached.

The days were wearing away quickly. One day a pilot braved our rocky airstrip en route back to Kotzebue. Had he seen any caribou? The answer

was not what I wanted to hear. He had not seen a single caribou in his flying the last couple of days. As I relay in the chapter about caribou, I did indeed shoot a bull that day, which was a total surprise to everyone.

One day Wayne and I still hunted some dark timber and found a young bull at a wallow, but he was not big enough. A few minutes later, we encountered three cows and a bull that we never got a good look at. He, he . . . just disappeared like an apparition. I felt pretty confident he was a big one, but not confident enough to shoot.

The second to last day of moose season, with the rivers and streams flooding beyond their banks, we decided to hunt the area downriver and behind camp; actually it was the only potential moose habitat left to hunt. About two miles from camp, Wayne found a fresh moose bed, which was still warm to the touch. Working our way up a brushy draw toward a ridge, we found an area where two bulls had very recently been fighting. The ground and trees within about a 50-yard circle were torn up, hair was scattered about and we even found about a 3-inch broken off tine.

Wayne suggested we get up where we could see as quickly as possible; thus, we started working our way up a ridge. About halfway to the crest, we had a pretty good view of the two little valleys below. We spotted the bull's antlers at about the same time. A quick look through my binoculars showed the bull had four brow points on one side, making him legal. I thought perhaps he was over 50 inches wide (which was required in that particular area for a bull to be legal). The bull was bedded in the draw directly below us.

After a quick conference I decided to get as close as possible to make my shot. Wayne would stay up top and direct me with hand signals if I needed help. Before heading down I made careful note of the location of the draw he was in. As I started dropping down the side of the ridge I realized the wind would be blowing from the moose to me if I dropped farther down and then walked up the draw toward the bull.

The stalk was a relatively easy one and along the way I found numerous moose beds, thankful-

Alaskan guide Wayne Taylor examines a recently vacated moose bed to see if it's still warm.

ly empty of cows, tracks and scrapes. I moved along very slowly occasionally glassing Wayne to see if I needed to make any adjustments. Apparently the bull was still bedded.

Then there he was. I could see his antler tips. He was looking away from me. Thus I eased around very slowly and cautiously. Thankfully, the softly falling rain and wet vegetation made the movement easier. I could see the bull's body. He was lying fully broadside to me. Slowly I raised the .30-06 Encore handgun, rested it on the crossed shooting sticks and aimed in the area of the bull's heart and lungs, then gently pulled the trigger. At the shot, I immediately reloaded. Surprisingly the bull made no effort to get up. Quickly I held the crosshairs this time on his neck and pulled the trigger. The bull slumped forward and never again moved. He was mine!

As I stood admiring the bull's antlers and his absolutely monstrous body, Wayne walked down to where we were. After hearty congratulations we shot several rolls of film and then measured the spread. It was almost 59 inches. Then came the hard work of quatering, carrying and then later returning for the skull and cape. Thank goodness we had a day and a half to pack him back to camp. We were able to do so just in time for me to catch the bush plane to Kotzebue and then a day later to Anchorage and home.

Alaskan moose had been far from easy. My bull was a good one, but one of these days I'll return to Alaska to hunt a 60-inch or better bull. And if I'm so fortunate to do so, I'm going to be darn sure there are several packers in camp and I can guarantee you, I'll not shoot one two miles from camp ever again!

Larry Weishuhn with his Alaskan moose taken in the northern reaches of the Brooks Range in Alaska on a hunt arranged by Henry Clark. The bull's palmate antlers were nearly 60 inches wide.

CHAPTER 13

CARIBOU: MISSING THE HERDS

PREVIOUS PAGES:
A de Havilland Otter floatplane taxies toward a rough-hewn landing stage on a lake in the Nunavik region of northern Quebec. Floatplanes are the air taxis of Quebec's caribou country and are a vital means of transportation in Canadian wilderness areas.

Hunter Denver McCormick searches for caribou in stunted black spruce of northern Quebec's forest-tundra. The area is within the range of the George River caribou herd, Canada's largest population of barren ground caribou.

othing to caribou hunting, pronounced an acquaintance at the Dallas Safari Club Convention where I had been a seminar speaker. "You simply sit on a ridge overlooking a river or lake crossing, or sit on a high hill and wait for the caribou to come past you. The hardest thing is to determine which one you want to shoot. I've journeyed to the northern tundra country several times and never failed to see hundreds of caribou bulls!" "There really is nothing to hunting caribou, it's a slam dunk!" he repeated.

A couple of weeks later I called Siegfried Gagnon, who was with Tourisme Quebec. I had met Siegfried earlier and, since he was involved with the tourism department of Quebec, he seemed to be the right person to call regarding a caribou hunt. As we visited and discussed my plans, I mentioned that I had never hunted caribou before but had gotten the go-ahead from my editors to write several articles if I could manage to slay one of the nomadic deer of the tundra.

I explained to Siegfried that my experience with caribou was limited. The only time I had been around them was several years before when I spent six weeks in the eastern region of Canada's Northwest Territories. On that visit to the Canadian tundra I had helped to band 26,000 geese. It was likely that we had seen an equal number of caribou, part of a herd that migrated up and down the western shore of Hudson Bay. Unfortunately, my stay had ended before caribou season began. Ever since then I had a hankering to hunt this most beautiful of the deer species.

Siegfried suggested that I call him back in about two weeks. By then he should have something set up for me. It so happened that I was headed to Las Vegas for a North American Hunting Club Jamboree at about the same time I was supposed to place the call to Quebec. One evening while at the Jamboree I happened to sit down in a small bar next to a friendly individual, who soon introduced himself as Denver McCormick. I immediately recognized him as someone who had attended my seminar. We started talking about hunting and it didn't take long for the subject of caribou to come up. Denver, like me, badly wanted to hunt caribou.

When I mentioned my plans to go to Quebec if I could get something set up later in the year, Denver mentioned that if I needed a partner, he would love to go. We continued visiting throughout the rest of the get-together and parted good friends. A couple of days later I spoke to Siegfried who had been in touch with Jack Hume, an old hand at caribou outfitting and an outfitter about whom I had heard a great deal of "good stuff."

A couple of days later Denver and I were booked on a caribou hunt in Quebec. During the interim I read all I could about caribou, about their habits, and how to judge a good set of antlers. Finally the day arrived. I met Denver in Montreal, had dinner and, next morning, headed to the airport for the flight to Schefferville, from where we would take a floatplane to our outback camp. Joining us in camp was a young couple from near Millinocket, Maine. All of us were full of anticipation and great hope.

The camp caretaker and ace boat "driver" took Denver and me to the far end of the lake on which we were camped and, under overcast skies, dropped us off with the promise to return and pick us up near dark. Denver and I walked up the rolling incline and found a big rock that would hide us from the wind. From our vantage point we could glass much of the surrounding country. Almost immediately we spotted a huge herd of caribou, including one of the better Quebec/Labrador sub-species bulls I've ever seen in real life or in photos. The problem was, he was probably over a mile and a half away and across the lake. All we could do was keep an eye on him, and alternately glass our side of the lake in hope of seeing another herd within stalking range. There were no caribou on our side however. When darkness came we walked back to the lakeshore and were ferried back to camp.

At first light we returned to the same place that we had hunted the evening before. Denver stayed closer to the lake while I headed farther inland where I could

The author watches for caribou on a snow-covered hillside. Weather in Canada's far north can change without warning, one moment clear, the next cloudy and snowing.

watch greater expanses of the barrens. I crawled into a little thicket of evergreen, which gave me some protection from the wind and rain but still afforded an excellent view of my surroundings. About two hours into the hunt I spotted a small herd of caribou moving below me, headed directly toward Denver. While I could see they were all bulls, I could tell little else. Ten minutes later I heard a shot, then a few moments later a second shot, then about three or so minutes later a third shot. Each sounded like solid hits as best as I could tell. If Denver had connected, and I felt assured he had, he was going to need some help, caping and boning the meat for the trip back to the water's edge.

I left my outpost and headed toward where I had left him. As I approached the rock where he had been hiding, I spotted his orange vest about 300 yards below and on the edge of the narrow band of timber that surrounded the lake. When he saw me he waved and I headed his way. "I got 'em!" he said with a wide smile and then pointed just below on the next level. I reached out with an extended hand of congratulations. Indeed he had gotten him, a truly nice representative of the Quebec/Labrador subspecies with a wide shovel and good bez points.

As I stood admiring Denver's caribou bull he said, "If you like this one, wait'll you see the other one. He's a bit bigger with good double shovels." We walked about a hundred yards while Denver told me his story. "I spotted them coming a long way off; you probably saw them too. They were headed directly toward me and then started angling toward the lake. I thought the best thing for me to do was to move in their direction before they got too close, so I headed toward the lake. About the time I got there I saw that they were about halfway between me and the spot I had just left, but still in range. I got a good rest and shot what I thought was the biggest. He went down but then tried to get up, so I shot him again. When he went down for good I started walking toward him. About the time I reached his side I looked back toward the lake and saw the bull with the double shovel. I really had no intention of shooting both of my bulls today, but when I saw that double shovel that was all it took. I'd read about those kinds of bulls and knew I wanted one." About that time we reached Denver's second bull. He was indeed a beauty.

Meat for the table. Ptarmigan taken after Larry Weishuhn fitted his Encore action with a 20-gauge shotgun barrel. These ptarmigan still display part of their brown summer plumage.

After taking photos we both started working on the capes and boning out the meat. By the time we finished the second one it was time to head to water's edge and wait for the boat to pick us up. While we deboned and caped, I kept a lookout for other caribou, but none were seen. That night there was a bit of a celebration in camp as I fried fresh caribou loin. We hung the rest in the fly-proof meat "shed."

On the next morning I returned to the same area, bolstered by the fact that the camp caretaker said many a bull had been taken where I hunted and sooner or later a big bull would wander by. The part I forgot to ask him was when. I hunted all day long, but never saw a single caribou. Back at camp I learned the young couple had seen no more than I had.

The next day was a repeat of the previous one, another caribou-less day. That night it snowed and continued snowing the following day. After being delivered to the shore on the far side of the lake I started roaming, covering large areas of the barrens. About noon I ran into the young couple; like me they had not seen a thing other than an orphaned calf and some beautiful country. We sat on a hillside eating an icy peanut butter sandwich and talked about the orphaned calf. The couple mentioned they had seen wolf tracks and

the young lady was concerned about the calf. Her husband mentioned the wolves would likely take the calf very shortly. About then, I got to thinking about how tender a caribou calf's venison would be, and how were just about out of meat due to the fact a plane had picked up Denver's meat and carried it back to Schefferville.

The more I thought about the calf, the more I thought about how we needed more meat in camp, and the wolves could probably go meat shopping elsewhere. You guessed it; I talked myself into the hunting the calf. The young couple took me to where they had last seen it. And sure enough it was still there. I laid down, got a good solid rest and squeezed the trigger on my .300 Win Mag T/C Encore rifle. Down went the calf.

By the time I had removed all the meat from the carcass, it was getting late. There was just enough room in my backpack for all the meat from the calf. I rolled the meat in the skin and stuck it in my pack and headed back toward the lake. It was late that night when I finally finished frying about half of the meat I had collected earlier that day. I'm not sure, but I think the camp caretaker ate about half of his body weight in meat. Even though I had prepared it, I'll have to say it was mighty tasty! During my forays for caribou, Denver hunted ptarmigan around camp and managed to bag several. Between caribou "veal" and ptarmigan we ate like kings. Before long the hunt was coming to an end and it was just as well. For whatever caribou there had been in the area had long since left. We left richer in experience and with a new respect for the barrens of Quebec, yet also with a yearning to return.

And return we did the following year. Once again Denver came north with me and again we hunted with Jack Hume. Our arrival in Schefferville was an interesting one, because when we landed you could hardly see from the plane to the

Never give up — this bull was taken on the last day of the hunt on a sandy river bottom.

INSET:
Using antlers for shoulder straps, the author packs out his last-day bull after stripping the velvet from its antlers.

The author with his first Quebec barren ground caribou; not a big bull by any means but one of the largest seen up to that point, with one day remaining in the hunt.

small terminal. Nonetheless, Hume's bus was waiting for us. On board we were introduced to Hilda and Leroy Wagner and two brothers from Maine, all four of who would be hunting with Denver and me.

We unloaded at Jack's lake-side camp and walked to the headquarters room. Jack greeted us and said the good news was that the caribou were moving in the right direction. The bad news was we were grounded until the fog moved out of the area. When queried how long that would be, his answer was "I hope soon . . ." But he didn't sound to promising.

We spent the next five days in Jack's base-camp. There was little to do but read and laze about, then go eat moose burgers at the nearby moose burger joint, come back and read the same magazines and books we had already read the day before. But that didn't dampen our spirits. Denver and I recounted tale after tale of great stags stalked, some which were bested and some which bested us. When we were not telling hunting stories, Denver told tales about his "many ex-wives." I'll admit he's a darn good storyteller, because I knew he had not been married nearly as often as what he made all those in camp believe. During one of those days in Schefferville, we did attempt to get to the hunting camp and we almost made it. But then had to turn back when you could not tell up from down, even flying just barely above the tundra.

Finally the call came — the fog was breaking, hurry up and get to camp. Waiting for us onshore was a party anxious to get out of camp, complete with many nice caribou racks. This was starting to look pretty good. According to those leaving camp, the caribou had been coming through quite regularly. Spirits were high! When the plane left we headed into the barrens, Denver and I went one way, Leroy and Ms. Hilda another and the two brothers a third way. When we all returned home that night we compared notes. No one had really seen much in the way of caribou, only one small herd of cows and calves. But caribou country, where moments before there was only caribou moss and open space, can suddenly be filled with wandering caribou herds. Surely the morrow would bring caribou. That night after supper I took store of what we had in the way of camp meat and noticed there was too little for the number of people in camp. Later that evening, I announced that, given an opportunity, I would shoot a meat bull tomorrow.

My chance came about midmorning. The young bull was a long way off, and it would give me an opportunity to stretch my .30-06 T/C Encore barrel. Taking a solid rest, I squeezed the trigger on the bull, I guessed a bit over 400 yards away. I heard the solid "whomp" of the bullet striking meat. After photos, I started the deboning process and about an hour later had the bull completely deboned, in meat sacks and was on my way back to camp with the meat. I didn't realize how lucky my decision was. Because that was the last caribou we saw for several days.

Finally with one day left to hunt, we got a radio message that a pilot was coming in to move us to a river crossing about five miles from camp. He would drop two of us off at each sand bar and then, later that afternoon, pick us up for the return flight. Leroy and Denver were dropped off first, then the plane returned and picked up the two brothers, and later returned to pick up Ms. Hilda, the camp caretaker who would serve as her guide, and me. About 20 minutes later, he dropped us off on a long sand bar. Flying in we had seen numerous caribou, but mostly on the wrong side of the river. I hoped some of those bulls would journey our way, because they possessed some impressive racks. Ms. Hilda and her guide went one way and I went the other. Straightaway I started seeing caribou, but mostly young bulls and cows. I heard a shot a few minutes later and knew Ms. Hilda had taken a bull.

I moved on down the river to an obvious crossing marked by many tracks. I sat down where I could see a great expanse of the river bottom. Almost immediately I spotted a bull walking my way, a lone bull that looked wide and big. He kept coming and finally stopped about 300 yards from where I was hidden. There he lay down. "He's my ace in the hole. If nothing else shows, he's mine!" I whispered to the mosquitoes buzzing around me. I searched up and down, in front and behind, a few caribou came by — all cows or young bulls. Far across the river I could see a big herd paralleling the river but they showed no sign of coming my way. The afternoon wore on and I knew that in less than an hour the plane would be returning for us. I continued to watch the bedded bull. His tops were nice, and his bottoms lacking, but he looked wide and he did have a very white neck. I was in a quandary. Should I wait longer or take the bull in front of me.

Then down the river I saw six bulls heading my way. They were nice but nothing special. They kept walking toward the bedded bull. As they reached where he lay, he stood up. The bedded bull stood a good 6 inches taller than the others. That was all I needed to convince me to take him. Quickly I set up my crossed shooting sticks, held the crosshairs of the Encore rifle where I wanted to hit the bull and pulled the trigger. I loaded a new round and shot the bull a second time. He took a couple of steps and fell.

It took three rushed trips to get the meat, head and cape to the agreed point. On the last trip with the meat, I spotted Ms. Hilda and her guide carrying meat and rack as well. I shouted my congratulations. She had indeed taken a dandy, and certainly the prettiest caribou I had seen in all of Quebec. That night in camp as we prepared to pack for the morning's flight back to Schefferville, I admired the caribou taken by our party. All of us had taken good bulls. Denver's bull lacked top points but had great shovels and bezes. Leroy's bull was equally gorgeous, but Ms. Hilda had taken the prize; her bull's rack was undoubtedly the most beautiful of the bunch.

One of these days I'm going to follow the hunter's moon back to northern Quebec, to hunt a truly outstanding caribou bull, one with great numbers of points on his tops and bezes, and double shovel and bezes that look like grain scoops. I know one's waiting for me up there somewhere and sooner or later I'll find him.

Packed and ready to go, Larry Weishuhn waits for the float-plane for a return flight to Schefferville. Packing for a northern caribou hunt requires careful planning with gear limited to the essentials.

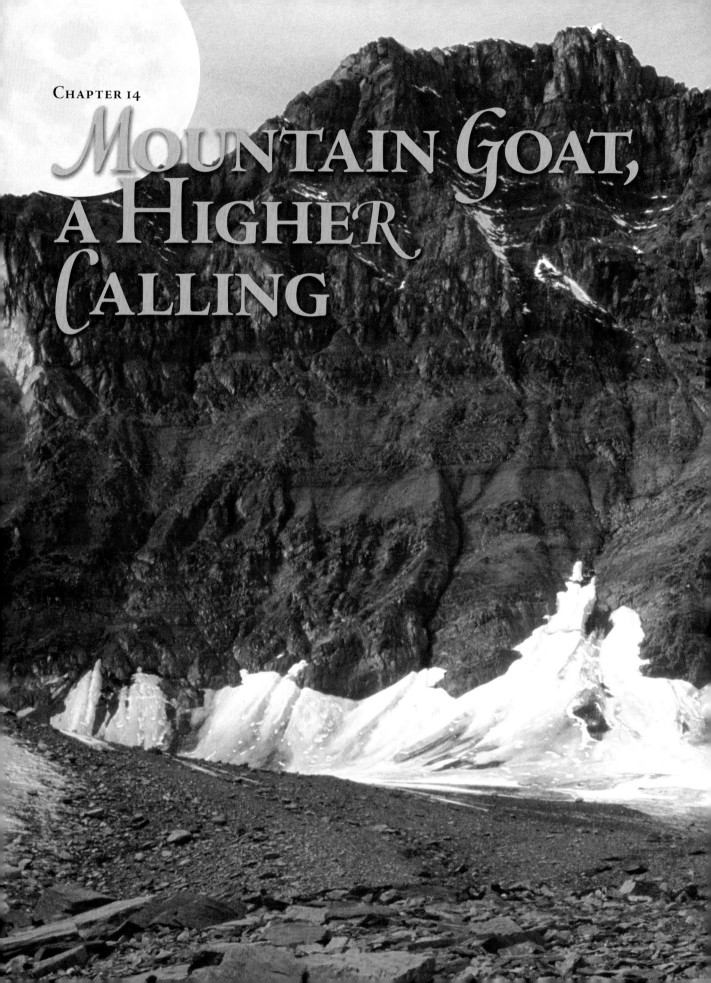

CHAPTER 14

MOUNTAIN GOAT, A HIGHER CALLING

See that speck of white against the gray walls on the left side of the glacier at the far end of the canyon?" queried Tom Vince, my guide. Instead of looking for the white speck I first looked at Tom. He was looking through a 30X spotting scope. I lowered my 10X binoculars and started digging through my pack to find my personal spotting scope. If the goat was a mere speck looking through his high-powered scope, my binoculars were going to be of little use. Moments later I had my Swarovski spotting scope set up and was looking in the general direction Tom's scope was aimed. "Seen it yet?" he asked. Just then I saw what he was looking at. "How many days is it going to take for us to get there?" I asked Tom.

"No use trying today," he commented without taking his eye away from his spotting scope, "we'll start out before first light in the morning, ride as far as we can and then make the crawl from there." "Since there appears to be only one goat, chances are pretty good it's an old billy. If there were several in the immediate area I'd suspect they were nannies and kids." Then, after about a 10-second pause he asked, "You game to try for him? We've got one full day and possibly part of another to get you a goat before we have to get out of here. Talked to base camp early this morning, Kevin said there's a storm headed this way, and if we don't get out by plane day after tomorrow, we'll have to ride back to camp and trail the horses with us. That shouldn't take more than a couple of days, if we're lucky! Short of that we'll be here for another week or so before we'll be able to get out."

We continued glassing the distant mountain slopes of the Muskwa River drainage. Far up one of the side canyons I could see two moose, a mediocre bull and a cow. In another high draw I spotted a small bull elk squiring his harem onto a relatively open ridge where he could keep an eye on fickle cows. In the canyon this side of the elk I spotted a small herd of mountain caribou moving across a relatively open slope.

I blinked my eyes, scarcely believing what I was seeing. I knew from its reputation that the northern portion of British Columbia, and especially the Prophet-Muskwa area, was a haven for big game, but until I saw it with my own eyes, I never imagined it would be as great. Earlier in the week, I had taken a fabulous 6 by 6 bull elk, described in an earlier chapter. Since that first success, Tom and I had crawled around various side canyons looking for a sizable moose or goat. Actually I was more interested in a mature goat than a bull moose. But just in case we saw "'Ol Moze," I had a western Canadian moose tag in my pocket as well.

We knew there was a big bull moose in the expansive canyon, because the day after I shot my elk, my hunting partner, Remington's Al Russo, had found an absolute monster while looking for a bull elk. Unfortunately Al did not have a moose tag. In spite of all our walking, crawling and glassing, Tom and I failed to see the big bull. Still, we had found several other bulls, but found a reason not to shoot any of them. Al and his guide, along with camera-

PREVIOUS PAGES:
Rocky Mountain goat country in the rugged eastern slopes of the northern Rockies of northwestern British Columbia. The terrain is steep, treacherous and absolutely breath-taking.

Guide Tom Vince glasses distant hillsides for goats while heading into the back country of the Muskwa River drainage.

man Punky Rose, had flown back to base camp where they would have a better chance at an elk. That left just Tom and me in camp.

When we had arrived, most of the vegetation had been a verdant green but over the course of several days, the greens had turned to yellows and brilliant reds. The mountains were now washed in brilliant colors and winter was on its way. As the afternoon wore on, Tom and I spotted two more specks of white in the general vicinity of the first goat, all three specks looked to be of equal size, possibly three billies. While walking back to our drop-camp we crossed a set of sizable grizzly tracks. They were fresh. We were not the only hunters on the prowl.

Back at camp we prepared the last of the elk loin from my bull – not only were we running out time, but groceries as well. Tomorrow would have to be the day if there was going to be a Rocky Mountain goat making the trip back to Texas with me. Sleep came easily, but was interrupted during the night as I dreamed of scaling the bluffs to be able to get within shooting range of the goats. When Tom stirred and started the coffee, I was ready to rise and, hopefully before the day was over, shine.

Seated in the rubble left by a retreating glacier, Larry Weishuhn searches the steep slopes of a high mountain valley for goats. Rocky Mountain goats live in rugged areas above the timberline up to a height of around 11,000 feet.

While I prepared the last of our bacon, Tom headed out to saddle horses. I wondered if the grizzly tracks we had seen not far from camp belonged to a bear that might now be getting a whiff of the frying bacon aroma. I imagined 'ol Ephram picking up his head and drawing deeply upon the breeze that carried the unique aroma, then turning to head in our direction.

Outside Tom talked to the horses in a reassuring manner, perhaps they smelled the bear. Horses saddled, Tom came back in the little Quonset hut we called camp. He commented on the bear tracks and how the horses acted a bit spooked. As he gathered his gear he commented, "Better take an extra sandwich today, it could be well after dark before we get back in tonight. It's going to take us quite a while to get to where we saw the goats, and then I suspect the climb and stalk could take us the rest of the day. But with any good luck at all, and if the goats haven't moved we should be able to get you within shooting range before the day's over." I grabbed my pack, stuffed in a couple of extra sandwiches and candy bars, knowing we were going to be in the saddle for quite sometime. Normally I had been skipping the candy bars because I would take energy from the plentiful blueberries, one of the true pleasures of hunting the Far North!

Alternately we rode and walked our horses toward the head of the long and

Tom Vince watches three goats on the slopes high above, having abandoned binoculars for a more powerful spotting scope.

broad canyon where we had scoped the goats. We had a bit of excitement when, in total darkness, we rode into a couple of animals, thinking they might be the grizzly whose tracks we had seen the evening before. There was some loud questioning our horses' ancestry and that of whatever was hidden in the darkness! When things were really getting a bit western, Tom produced a flashlight and lit up two moose cows. By first light we were well on the way. Gradually the canyon narrowed and the walls on either side got steeper and steeper. By noon we were aproaching the area where we thought the goats had been feeding on the gray slate slope. Then, as we rounded a huge boulder, there they were; three goats about a mile away and about 300 or 400 yards apart. We dismounted, tied the horses and set up Tom's spotting scope. Moments later Tom spoke, "All three are billies, the biggest is the last one on the left." Looking about at the terrain he again spoke, "Think we'll unsaddle the horses here, tether them, and go on, on foot." He continued, "We're going to have to take it slow and steady. Looks like we'll have to crawl up, then past the first two goats to get to the third and biggest one, slow and steady gets the goat!" I didn't know about the first part, but I did like the idea of slow and steady. After unsaddling my horse, I ate a sandwich and then repacked my daypack to include only some extra ammunition for my .300 Remington Ultra Mag, my knife, a short coil of rope, a couple of rolls of film and my camera. I stashed the rest of my gear under my saddle.

The first couple of hundred yards were extremely steep, but were obligingly covered with hip-high brush that made convenient handholds. For the first hundred or so yards, we were out of sight of the goats and could partially stand up when we moved. After that, it was a different story entirely, because then we were exposed to them – that meant crawling through the bushes like a snake. Tom was ahead and kept looking at the goats with his binocs. Each time they looked our way we froze, trying not to slide back down the mountain.

Occasionally we were able to take advantage of the slope and boulders, which hid us from view. I noticed that the bushes were getting shorter and, looking up, I noticed that we would soon be out of cover, at which point things were going to get extremely "interesting." Each time we slowed or stoped I could hear Tom say, "Slow and steady gets the goat!" I think it was more of an encouragement to me than anything else. I also noticed each time I looked up that it appeared we were crawling directly in line with the sun.

Larry Weishuhn levels his rifle, loaded with .300 Remington Ultra Mag, at a goat over 500 yards away. Rugged conditions and the difficulty of approaching nearer to the quarry demanded a long-range shot.

Guide Tom "slow and steady gets the goat" Vince and the author pose with their long-shot goat. For Larry Weishuhn the 9-incher was, in many ways, the trophy of a lifetime.

"Don't move; the first goat is directly above us, he's looking down at us," whispered Tom. I tried to do my best lichen-on-a-rock imitation. "He hasn't seen us. I think he's just gotten up to stretch. He's not one we're interested in, looks like he's got about 7 inches of horn. The biggest one is at least nine." Moments seemed like hours. Then, finally, the goat moved back from the edge of the rock he had been bedded on, and our assault on the mountain continued. We would crawl a few steps, taking advantage of all the cover possible, then wait while the goat looked our way.

The next obstacle was the second goat, as if the slopes we were on weren't enough of a challenge. By taking advantage of a narrow ridge, we were able to move parallel along the side of the mountain to get past him, but in doing so that put us pretty much in an open area, possibly making us visible to our goat. Our goat was alternately feeding and then laying down. The problem was that when he laid down he did so on a small alcove which placed him to look directly in our direction. That did not, however, stop us from moving, but at a pace that would have made a snail seem to move with the speed of a hare.

"We've got two options," said Tom in a low whisper, "We can drop back down the slope and try to move parallel below that ridge (pointing to a narrow ridge about a hundred yards below and to our left). If we do that, we can probably cut the range down to about 300 yards eventually. It'll get us closer, but it will also take us another hour or so. Or, we can try to make it to that rill up ahead which will likely put us within about 500 yards of him, and save us a bunch of time. It's your call?"

I looked at the ridge below, and didn't like the idea of losing altitude or eating up more time. I remembered having shot the .300 RUM at the bench at 500 yards and knew if I could get a solid rest, I'd be able to hit my target. "Let's make it to the rill and try to get up to the same level as the goat. I can kill him from there." The goat apparently spotted or heard something above him, stood up and stared upward. Immediately, Tom and I crawled as fast as we could to the rill that would provide us some more protection.

Ten minutes later we were on the same level as the goat. In the rill I found a comfortable place from which to attempt the shot. I set up my backpack as a rest but found that I was staring through the scope directly at the sun. I maneuvered around a bit, hoping to change the angle slightly. No matter what I did, the rifle was pointed toward the sun. Based on the sun's angle and descent, it would be at least an hour or so before I would not be staring into it when I made the shot. That would be too much time, and if the goat moved much in any direction I would lose sight of him.

What to do? I squinted to relieve some of the glare. I held the crosshairs above the goat at what I deemed an appropriate amount to allow for bullet drop, whispered a prayer and tugged the trigger. Before I could chamber a second round I heard Tom say, "You hit him about where the front legs meet the body, shoot again." This time I held a bit higher and pulled the trigger. Again I heard Tom say, "You hit him this time a bit higher. He's going down. If you can, get another into him to anchor him where he is; we don't want him to fall off the bluff." My third shot took him squarely through both shoulders and he went down. I loaded in a fourth round and fired; that one hit his left hip. The goat lay still. He was down and dead. Had I not known how my rifle shot at that range, I would not have attempted the shot, but I had previously fired several times at 500 yards and beyond and knew where the bullet should hit at that distance.

With the goat down, Tom took off at a fast pace. Me? I walked and crawled slowly toward where my white prize lay. After all, the ground between me and the goat was steeper and more treacherous than any I had encountered while getting to within 500 yards of him. I finally arrived where Tom sat at the goat's side; my pants torn, sweated totally wet, but filled with joy. My mature billy was indeed a prize worth pursuing. His dark horns, all 9 inches of them, contrasted with his solid white coat of hair. He was a handsome rascal. By the time we completed taking photos, skinning the cape and taking what worthwhile meat there was, darkness was not that far away, and we were still a mile away from our horses and many miles from camp. The crawl down the hill was as treacherous as had been the crawl up. Several times we had to backtrack to find an easier and safer way down.

A slice of a hunter's moon shone high above the eastern side of the canyon as we saddled our horses for the ride back to camp. Tired but happy we headed home. Slow and steady had gotten the goat and slow and steady would take us back to camp, barring an encounter with a grizzly...

Chapter 15

Addicted to Red Stags

Paul Bamber, owner of Wanganui Safaris, located in New Zealand's remote Wanganui River Valley, walked onto the deck of the lodge where I paced back and forth, staring at steep-sided valleys filled with dense fog just below the deck's edge. In the distance I heard the roar of a red stag, which sounded to me more like the bray of a lovesick Brahman bull than a call made by a deer. I raised my right arm and pointed. Paul just smiled, then spoke in his New Zealand brand of English, "Anxious, are you? Not to worry, the fog will lift soon enough and we will venture forth to see about getting you a proper stag. They've just started their roaring season. Much more masculine sound than your elk, wouldn't you say so?"

Before I could answer Travis and Dawn Simpson along with Irvin and Wendy Barnhart stepped onto the deck as well. All four had hunted the world, occasionally together, and they listened intently to the roar of the stags. The Down Under adventure was return engagement for them. Knowing that they had hunted with Paul Bamber in the past and were now back to hunt with him again, made me all the more excited about the hunt. "I guess you are all ready to go hunting?" asked Bamber. "I'll get the guys to prepare for the day's hunt." I didn't know about the rest of my anxious cohorts, but I wanted to applaud. While the rest of my group walked back inside to prepare their gear, I stayed on the deck and listened to the roaring of the stags, just as I had done the evening before after everyone else had gone to bed. They did indeed sound more masculine and impressive than our elk!

About an hour later we were headed to the back part of the Wanganui property where the day before Mark Haynes and Chris Joll, Wanganui's ace guides, had located several good stags in the 300 to 320 SCI score range. I wanted to take one that would score in the silver medal range, not that I cared much about the score, but I knew such a stag would indeed be impressive. Wendy and Dawn hoped to take a much larger stag, suffice it to say here, they eventually did score on such stags. Wendy's scored in the 390s and Dawn's in the 340s. Irvin was after a non-typical stag this trip. His like mine didn't come easy!

On our first evening in camp Paul had explained that Wanganui had been in his family for several generations and dated back to the days when red stags and other antlered and horned ungulates were first released in New Zealand. Wanganui can best be described as luxurious, complete with deep, steep-sided canyons, all of which are covered in a wide variety of vegetation typical of New Zealand's verdant flora. This bit of heaven on earth is an ideal habitat for red stag, sika and fallow deer, as well as wild hogs and goats. If there were a more attractive and game-productive property on New Zealand's North Island, it would be a miracle.

OPPOSITE:
Larry Weishuhn took this magnificent 6-by-7 Wanganui red stag with his .30-06 Encore. Red stags, a large European deer similar to Elk, were introduced to New Zealand in the 1850s.

Three red stags head up a ravine in the remote Wanganui River Valley on New Zealand's North Island. A relative of the elk, red deer were introduced to New Zealand from Great Britain.

I had wanted to hunt in New Zealand ever since I had read an article by Warren Page in Field & Stream that described how he had hunted red stags in the island's mountains. That hunting story lit a flame that had burned for years before I was finally able to arrange a New Zealand hunt for myself, thanks in part to Travis Simpson and the graciousness of Paul Bamber. Travis, an occasional hunting partner, also served as my cameraman for my Outdoor Channel television show, "Hunting the World." Together, we hoped to film my hunt for a couple of red stags as well as a hunt for chamois on the South Island.

When the fog finally lifted we were ready to go after stags! We traveled to the area where Mark and Chris had seen good stags the day before. We glassed some promising areas and spotted several red stags, but not quite with the antler size we were looking for. After searching several canyons and hillsides, Mark and I took off walking along a road that side-hilled the steep-sided canyon walls. We soon spotted one of the stags he had seen the day before. He was far across a deep canyon and, had it not been that less than six weeks since I had major back surgery, you could not have stopped me from trying to stalk closer. I knew my physical limitations, however, and the last thing I wanted to do was to cause further problems with my back. We sat down and waited, hoping the stag would indeed come our way.

Wanganui Safaris' Mark Haynes (left) guided the author to this absolutely beautiful 9 by 8 red stag.

Travis manned the camera while we started glassing not only "my" stag but also several other promising stags and a huge sika in the canyons below us. As the morning wore on, "my" stag finally started moving downhill all the way to the bottom of the canyon. My prayers were being answered, especially when the

stag started coming our way, even though his pace was considerably slower than what I had hoped for. Occasionally he would stop and roar, announcing his presence to the world.

It was all I could do to sit there and wait. My mind wanted to make the stalk, but my body, with its lower back encased in a body brace, protested any move that my surgeon might have described as unnecessary and stupid. Fortunately, my surgeon was also a hunter otherwise I doubt seriously that he would have consented to my traveling several thousands of miles to go on a steep mountain hunt so quickly after major surgery. So I waited for the stag to come my way. All the while I had my T/C Encore .30-06 rifle rested on shooting sticks, aimed at the stag.

"How far?" I asked Mark. "Mmmmm, likely close to 400 meters," said he, watching through the Swarovski spotting scope. "He's a good stag, great mass, good tops. If I were to slight him for anything it would be relatively short brows." "I like him and I want him," was my only reply. With that I glanced at Mark and by the expression on his face, I suspected he liked him as well.

The stag finally started moving at an angle toward us. "I know where this '06 will hit a target at 400 yards," I told Mark. "When he gets to that point, I'm going to shoot.

Larry Weishuhn prepares to take a shot at a distant stag using a nearby tree for a rest.

Besides the angle is steeply downhill, so the shot should actually be somewhat closer." I mentally calculated that the shot should be between 200 and 250 yards. When the bull stopped and turned broadside I gently pulled the trigger.

Mark watched through the Swarovski scope. "You hit him hard! Shoot again!" I did, and then again and again before he went down. As I pulled the last spent case out of the single-shot's barrel, I noticed Mark looking at me with a questioning expression on his face. "You made that single-shot sound like you were shooting an entirely different action," he said. I just smiled and blew the smoke out of the end of the barrel. That same Encore single-shot had helped me account for a lot of big game in many different terrains and habitats. Years of hunting with the same gun had helped me learn how to reload and shoot with it quicker than most hunters can work their bolt-action rifles.

The steep downhill walk to the stag was a bit difficult and trying. By the time we got to the old red deer's side, I was nearly done in. But not so much so that I couldn't reach down and run my hands over his fabulous antlers. They indeed were massive and had 9 points on one side and 10 on the other. I sat for a while simply admiring the stag's rack and the beauty of the area.

A couple of days later, after Dawn took her great stag and Wendy took an absolutely monstrous stag, Travis, Dawn, Mark and I headed to the South Island to hunt chamois. Inclement weather prevented us from doing much hunting, but I still

Larry Weishuhn with a chamois he took in the Southern Alps of New Zealand's South Island. The surefooted chamois' remote alpine habitat and its ability to run at 30 mph and leap 20-foot distances make it a challenging game animal to hunt.

managed to take an ancient female, with long, though rather thin horns. Then the weather got worse and we headed back to the North Island, where I hoped to take a second red stag.

That hunt was not an easy one, and several days passed before we found a stag that fit both my budget and my liking. Mark and I, followed by Travis with his camera, spotted four big stags on a distant slope. With a bit of careful stalking, we cut the distance to about 300 or so yards. One of the stags, with a massive 6 by 7 rack, finally offered a broadside shot. When all was properly aligned I gently tugged at the .30-06 Encore's trigger. A resounding "plop" echoed across the hills, the result of a solid hit. Before the stag could go down I reloaded and shot a second time, this time aiming where neck and shoulder meet. The shot was sound and I watched in awe as the stag tumbled spectacularly head over heals some 200 yards down the steep slope before coming to rest squarely on one of the property's roads. All the while (Mark told me later) I was saying aloud, "Please don't let him break his antlers." He didn't break any antlers, and once at his side it was easy to understand why. They were extremely heavy! I could not have been more pleased with my hunt for red stag with Wanganui Safaris. Before leaving I made arrangements to return in the future to again hunt the property's awesome red stags.

Shortly after my return, I received a call from Swarovski Optiks' Jim Morey. He had heard about my New Zealand trip from a mutual friend. "How would you like to join me on a red stag hunt in Austria for native, mountain stags?" Jim asked, "Swarovski Optiks just picked up the Radurschl Reserve, an area previously hunted by the Hapsburg family. It will be the trip of a lifetime. Care to go?"

I couldn't say "YES!" fast enough. When Jim told me the dates in early September, I hesitated then replied, "Jim, my wife, Mary Anne and I will be married 35 years September 4th; I doubt seriously I can get away then." "No problem," he replied, "bring her with you; I'll take my wife Leslie and we'll help ya'll celebrate in proper Austrian style." Before hanging up the phone, we worked out the details. We would first go to Innsbruck and then on to the Radurschl to hunt stags. While Jim and I hunted during the days, Mary Anne and Leslie would tour the region. That afternoon I made arrangements to have Herman Brune accompany us as a cameraman to record the hunt for my television show, "Hunting the World." Now all that we needed was for time to pass quickly. It did.

After clearing customs, we toured Innsbruck, including not only the tourist

Dawn Simpson with a huge stag taken on Wanganui Safaris' property on the same hunt with Larry Weishuhn. Dawn's husband, Travis, worked as the cameraman.

areas, but other parts seldom penetrated by travelers. These were the best of places, because they truly presented the Austrian charm. Then it was on to the Radurschl Reserve close to the Italian border, one of the few remaining pristine high alpine valleys in all of Europe.

The camp was a proper hunting lodge built for the Hapsburgs nestled high in the Alps. It was complete with excellent rooms, comfortable beds and unique wood stoves to keep the rooms warm. After stowing our gear and meeting the two resident gamekeeper/guides, Gerhard Maier and Franz Pinzer, Jim, Herman and I excused ourselves and headed to the rifle range. Jim's custom rifle was shooting exactly where it was supposed to. My well-traveled .30-06 T/C Encore rifle needed a bit of adjustment after the long journey, but after a couple of shots, I was dialed in. The afternoon passed quickly and that night we were treated to a most special meal prepared by one of the finest chefs in the world, Seppl Haueis. Sleep would have come easy had it not been for an overstuffed stomach.

Morning, as in any hunting camp, came early and after a quick scrumptious breakfast we headed into the mountains behind camp. Although I was prepared for mountain climbing, I was not quite prepared for the steepness of the mountains. Thankfully we walked slowly, setting up periodically to glass the alternately wooded

Wendy Barnhart, wife of Weatherby Award winner, Irvin Barnhart, with a 400-class stag taken on the same hunt.

and relatively open canyon walls. We soon spotted our first red deer, a group of mostly hinds, and then later a couple of chamois.

The chamois fascinated me. I had seen a couple on a previous trip to Austria, but on that occasion as on this one, chamois season was not open. I had however been fortunate to take one earlier in the year in New Zealand. Game populations on the Radurschl Reserve are closely monitored by gamekeepers Pinzer and Maier. They know the animals which live there intimately, and use biological data to determine exactly how many and, to a great extent, which animals should be taken each year. In addition to a scientific regimen involving harvest, they also make certain the animals are properly taken care of during the stress periods of winter, through administering supplemental feed.

Radurschl's game population consists of red deer, roe deer, chamois, Alpine ibex, as well as auerhahn or capercaillie and black grouse. With my background as a wildlife biologist involved in quality management and research, I was impressed by both Pinzer and Maier, and their knowledge and passion for the various species whose lives they oversaw. I was equally impressed with the reverence shown the animals we hunted, and especially how they were honored once taken. Equally impressive was how the people in that part of Austria felt about hunting and hunters. Once we had taken our game, hikers and locals stopped by to congratulate us for our good fortune. Their well wishes were genuine and honest, which was extremely refreshing. U.S. citizens could do well to learn from the European traditions regarding hunting and the high esteem that the general public holds for hunters.

The author with his magnificent 6 by 7 Austrian red stag taken on Swarovski's private Radurschl hunting reserve. Joining in the celebration are Jim Morey (left, rear) and Jaeger Gerhart Maier.

On our first afternoon in camp, Gerhart Maier, Herman and I headed to a hochsitz, or stand, in one of the luxuriant valleys that overlooked a timber cut that had grown up with a variety of deer food. Comfortably seated, it didn't take long for two great stags to appear, one obviously a couple of years younger than the other, but both impressive. I watched with great interest as they fed on the lush vegetation. "Larry, the von on de rite, he is an oldt stag. I tink you shouldt shoot him." spoke Gerhard in a stage whisper.

Up until that time I had merely admired the stags, hoping to have an opportunity at one of equal size, but knowing only particular animals are annually selected for harvest. When I heard Gerhart's instructions it was like someone had flipped a switch. Suddenly, I almost started shaking, partly out of excitement, and partly out of knowing

Larry Weishuhn's red stag was at least 10 years old. It is shown here with a Tyrolean hunter's hat decorated with an evergreen sprig as a token of a successful hunt.

INSET:
The leather-wrapped *Jagdhorn* or hunting horn is used to play a *tote*, a traditional call honoring the fallen prey.

I had to properly place the bullet. The last thing, as is always the case, I did not want to merely wound such a fabulous animal.

I peered through the Swarovski scope and found the stag, then planted the crosshairs firmly just behind the shoulder, but waited until he cleared a slight screening of brush before pulling the trigger. When finally I did, and I was also certain Herman was on the animal, I gently pulled the trigger. Immediately after the shot, I heard the solid, whomp of the bullet striking the animal, watched him run about 20 steps and fall. Before I could reload, Gerhart was congratulating me. A few moments later we started making our way across a small stream toward my Austrian mountain stag.

On the way, Gerhart broke off three evergreen branches and upon our arrival dipped each in the animal's blood. He placed one of the branches at the site where the bullet had struck the animal and placed a second branch, the *letztbissen* (or last bite) in the stag's mouth. Gerhart then removed his Tyrolean hat and placed it on the third branch and extended the branch to me along with his right hand and the salute of "Waidmannsheil." I accepted the branch with Waidmannsdank and then placed the branch on the right side of my Tyrolean hat. There the branch would remain for 24 hours to demonstrate my respect for the animal, but also to indicate my excellent fortune in taking a stag. Throughout the simple ceremony, there is great respect shown not only the animal but also the hunter and the great and long tradition of hunting! Like I said, we who live in the U.S.A. could learn a lot from our European hunting kinfolk!

My stag was one that Gerhart had been watching for several years and he later showed me the stag's shed antlers and how he had progressed in recent years. He was a sizable 6 by 7 with deep russet-colored antlers, including the tips. I noticed he was also smaller in body than the red stags I had encountered in New Zealand, but he was an animal of which I was most proud! That same afternoon Jim Morey, with his guide and gamekeeper Franz Pinzer, hunted a high mountain valley, where they encountered well over 50 stags. They shot a stag that afternoon, an extremely old animal, but one with massive antlers having 5 points on both sides. Jim's hunt had been equally exciting because it required squirming past lesser stags and hinds to get into position for a shot.

Needless to say that night was a rather long one, as everyone in camp regaled each other with tales of great stags won and lost. Long after our wives had headed to bed, the hunters stayed up toasting the great animals of Radurschl, the grand traditions of hunting, and the time spent with old and new friends. On the next afternoon, with the animals safely back at camp, a huge crowd of well-wishers joined us, and Jim played the proper and respectful *tote* (death song of honor) on his *Jaghorn* for the stags. Ah Austria! To some it may be alive with the sounds of music, but for me it will always be alive with the sights and sounds of hunting.

Garbed in traditional hunting costume, *Jaegers,* or huntsmen, of Austria's Radurschl Reserve examine the distant hillsides for red stags.

INSET:
The red stag's *letztbissen* — honoring the stag with his last bite — is one of the great hunting traditions in Austria.

CHAPTER 16

KUDOS FOR KUDU

Show me a hunter who has never dreamed of hunting in Africa, and I'll show you a liar. A pretty strong statement, I know, and while there may be some exceptions, I'd bet there are darn few. I was always someone who knew in the back of my mind that, one day, I would HAVE to go to Africa. I dreamed about it often, especially when reading Rurark and a few others. Craig Boddington, now a general in the Marine Corps, was also a great influence on my wanting to go to Africa. Craig and I had traveled together for several weeks back when we were both on the National Rifle Association's Great American Hunters' Tour. Every day I questioned him about his African exploits. Craig always answered my questions and did it in a manner that made me want to go all the more.

Finally, my dream became a reality when Kim Hicks (editor of *The Texas Hunting Directory*), Jay Novacek (formerly with the Dallas Cowboys, and, like Kim, part owner of the Texas Hunting Directory), Denver McCormick and his wife Linda (I'd hunted with Denver on several occasions) and I decided we should go to South Africa to hunt a variety of plains game. After a long visit with Brown Delozier, booking agent and a veteran of several African safaris, we decided to hunt in the Eastern Cape of South Africa with Barry Burchill's Frontier Safaris.

The flight from Miami to Cape Town was a long one, but since we were flying with several other hunting parties, the trip was more like a long hunting campfire session. A long boring flight turned into a party! From Cape Town we flew to Elizabethtown where we were met by Barry and his crew of professional hunters. I was immediately assigned a young man named Glen Ballintyne as my guide. Glen, I discovered, came from a long line of professional hunters and, in spite of his youth, was a consummate professional as well as an excellent hunting companion.

Camp was a luxurious set of bungalows set high on a hill overlooking a broad valley. Steps wound along the edge of the bluff to a kitchen area where hunters would gather nightly to discuss their day's activities. It didn't take long to stow gear and check our rifles after the long haul from Texas. I had brought three guns, a .44 Ruger Super Blackhawk Hunter, my .30-06 T/C Encore handgun and a .300 Win Mag custom-made Match Grade Arms rifle. During the course of the hunt I hoped to take animals with all three.

On the first afternoon, Denver, Linda, Glen and his right-hand man Walter and I headed to Glen's father's property where we hunted black wildebeest. The hunt proved successful with both Denver and I taking good representatives of the species, which was my goal, rather than looking for record-book animals. That night, before heading back to our camp, we had a couple glasses of wine with Glen's father and family as we were shown his nicely decorated trophy room. Two animals in particular caught my attention: an

OPPOSITE:
Silhouetted against the setting sun, a hunter trecks across the Karoo Plains of South Africa's Eastern Cape. South African sunsets are among the most beautiful in the world.

Professional hunter Glen Ballintyne, his tracker Walter and the author trail a kudu through the veldt in South Africa's Karoo Plains.

excellent Eastern Cape kudu and a bushbuck. I knew then that before my hunt was over, those were two animals I would have to do my dead level best to collect.

During a predawn breakfast, Glen suggested we hunt for kudu. I looked over at Denver and, like me, he was primed and ready. Shortly after first light, having walked a couple of miles, Glen stopped and pointed to an animal across a wide canyon. He raised his index finger to his lips to indicate silence, then made the shape of a spiraled horn with his hand. Next he pointed to me and indicated that I should get ready to shoot. I could not see a bull with horns, although I could see a couple of cows. I glanced up from where I sat to Glen, who was glassing the area. "Get ready, he's coming out!" whispered Glen. Just then I saw the spiral-horned bull step into view, quartering away from me. "Try to get him with a quartering shot through the last rib," instructed Glen.

When the crosshairs aligned where they should be, I pulled the trigger but just as I did I saw the kudu change angles. The shot hit the bull breaking his right hind leg. Quickly I locked in a second round but before I could fire, the kudu was gone. I knew immediately I had only wounded the bull, the last thing on earth I wanted to do. Immediately I felt bad for the animal. "We'll have to go find him!" said Glen, knowing the gravity of the situation. "Walter is a good tracker; we should be able to find him." "I'm sorry," I said apologetically, more to the animal than to Glen. "I should have waited for a better shot, but I thought I could slip one in behind his last rib and angle it into the vitals." Minutes later we stood where the kudu had been when it received the shot. A few steps farther we found blood. We waited a bit in hopes the bull would lie down and give me another shot, and then followed the blood trail and spoor.

Larry Weishuhn and his hunting partner, Denver McCormick, with Larry's first kudu taken on the first morning of the hunt in the Eastern Cape of South Africa.

The author poses with a nice Eastern Cape kudu, which has been cleaned up and pulled into the open. Mature bulls can weigh as much as 650 pounds.

We followed the trail for about a mile without getting another look at the animal. Then there was no blood. By looking closely, we could identify my wounded kudu from the others by noticing a slight drag in the prints of his hind foot. We continued on for nearly two miles. The wounded bull, along with three cows, was heading for higher ground. Hopefully by heading to higher ground myself I might get another shot at him.

The morning was starting to wear upon me, but we pushed on. Glen and I stayed on the trail while Walter headed to an area where he thought the kudu might go, a remote water hole. If he found him there, he would come back to get us and, hopefully, I could get a finishing shot into the bull. I felt really bad for the kudu. Missing an animal I don't mind, wounding him and causing him pain and misery is something I mind terribly. If I am going to kill an animal, I owe it to him to do the job quickly and humanely. I had failed and I didn't like it!

We continued on and I was beginning to question if indeed I had done much damage to the kudu, other than possibly a flesh wound that, sans infection, would heal. Still we continued on. By early afternoon we had covered several miles; some in a straight line, others in stretches of meandering through dense thorn thickets. Just when it seemed all was lost, Glen, who was about 6 feet ahead of me, raised his hand and then waved me forward, while pointing up ahead at something in the brush with his other hand. I eased forward slowly. There in the shadows of a bushy

Nyala are undoubtedly one of the most beautiful big game animals in the world. Larry Weishuhn took this one on Frontier Safaris' Eastern Cape reserve.

tree lay a kudu facing into the wind, thankfully looking away from where we stood.

Ever so slowly I raised my rifle, took aim and lightly touched the trigger. At the shot, the bull simply lowered his head. It was over! I had often read about the toughness and tenacity of African antelope, and this one had certainly proved the point! A lesser animal would have given up long before this one did.

The bull, typical of Eastern Cape kudu, was gray with brilliant white chevrons. He was extremely handsome! His horn length was probably about 44 or so inches, a nice representative of the species. Normally Eastern Cape kudu are not as big in body or horn size as some of their kindred. Looking at the results of my first shot, there was little doubt he would have recovered nicely. But I was tremendously glad we had continued the chase and I was finally able to finish what I had started.

On the way back to camp we spotted another kudu bull, about the same size as mine. Denver who had planned on taking two kudu bulls before the trip was over, opted to take this bull and did so after a short stalk and a single shot from his .30-338 Weatherby. That night there were several bottles of excellent South African wine opened in camp.

Over the next few days, Denver and I hunted several other species of antelope together, including nyala, my third most wanted antelope from South Africa. We even introduced Ms. Linda to big game hunting. After watching Denver and me and all the fun we were having, she decided she wanted to shoot an impala. She succeeded using my rifle. Later Denver told me, "I think YOU made a mistake by letting my wife take that impala. Ever since then she's been planning hunting trips to far off places!" I don't know, sounded perfect to me!

One morning while hunting bushbuck we encountered three kudu bulls high in the hills on a ranch adjoining Burchill's property. The horns on two of the bulls were likely about 46 or so inches long, and those on the third were easily 52 or 53 inches long, a fabulous Eastern Cape bull. We stalked to within about a hundred yards and debated whether or not to shoot another kudu that day. For reasons I'll never figure out, we decided to turn down the bull, perhaps because the following day we planned to head to a ranch several hours away, which had a reputation of producing monstrous kudus. Still, I've kicked myself many times for not taking the biggest of those three bulls!

The following morning we left well before first light, driving to a property that had a reputation for big kudu. We arrived there just as the sun was starting to peek over the horizon. We switched vehicles and drove into the rolling hills which reminded me greatly of the guajilla and blackbrush hills only a short distance below my southern Texas home. It was amazing how much this area of South

Surrounded by cactus and thorn country that resembled his native South Texas, the author poses with a fine Eastern Cape kudu.

Larry Weishuhn shot this bushbuck in the waning moments of his South African hunt.

Africa reminded me of Texas. Other than some of the succulents, many of the brush and tree species were quite similar to the vegetation of my home region.

Our hunting technique amounted primarily to driving to a promising area, then getting out and crawling to a vantage point to overlook the great expanse of bush. We also checked areas around windmills and water holes and spotted several kudu, but mostly lesser bulls. We did spot one gigantic bull whose head was partially hidden behind a rock outcropping. I got ready to shoot, waiting for Glen or the rancher to give me the go-ahead. They glassed and I looked through my scope. "Don't shoot!" came the command. "He's only got one horn. The good one is about 55 inches long, the other is broken off just above the base . . ." Too bad, such a long-horned bull would have looked good on my office wall back in Texas.

We continued the hunt and a couple miles farther spotted a bull high on a hill. "He's a good bull," Glen observed, "probably 46 or so, fairly narrow, but that could also make him longer. Care to try for him? We can probably find one better, but I think if we work it right we can get you into position and get good footage of him for the television show as well." Oh yeah, I forgot to mention that on this particular morning's hunt I was accompanied by an ESPN cameraman, to film a segment for a show Jay Novacek was hosting. The cameramen had accompanied Jay on all his hunts; now it was my turn.

Glen, the cameraman and I jumped off the back of the Toyota truck, took a look at the terrain and made a plan. By dropping back behind the hill, keeping the wind in our face and the sun quartering behind us, we should be able to cut the distance down to about 200 yards, as long as the kudu stayed where he was and we didn't

Denver McCormick with a huge Eastern Cape kudu, taken near the end of the hunt.

spook him by jumping several other kudu en route. There were a lot of "ifs" to consider, but the plan could work.

About 20 minutes, later we were in position, but the kudu wasn't! While we had been making our stalk, he had dropped off of the top of the hill and walked to the bottom of the canyon. There he bedded down in a forest of cactus and thorns. We had to change angles a couple of times but finally got a clear lane of fire, both for the camera and me. When all was set, I fired and the kudu pitched forward.

The walk down to the kudu was an "interesting one," especially when Glen casually observed: "Any other time you could not pay me enough to walk into this canyon." My questioning look prompted him to expand upon his statement. "This area is covered with cobras — big ones." My growing expression of terror prompted him to add soothingly, "But right now they're all denned up, no self-respecting cobra would be out once the weather cooled." It was a comforting thought, but the temperature that day was about 70 degrees Fahrenheit. Back home rattlesnakes that had been denned up would be back out sunning themselves. What about a non-self-respecting cobra? Thankfully there were no such cobras, at least not where I could see them.

The kudu bull had about 45-inch horns, and we took photos and called in the meat crew, who carried the un-gutted bull up a 500-yard-long steep incline, to load it onto the Toyota. After gathering up the crew, we headed around the next bend in the road, and spotted another kudu bull. "Shoot him!" came the instruction from the ranch owner. "He's over 50 and he's an old bull we've been hunting for over a year!"

Denver obeyed, and a couple of minutes later we walked up to a massive bull, with horns well over 50 inches long. Denver was tickled and I was well pleased for him. In a couple of hours we had taken two excellent Eastern Cape kudu. A great way to top off our first African hunt!

And yes, there was another hunting day, a day I will long remember. For before it was over, both Denver and I had also taken excellent bushbuck. Mine was an adventure I shall never forget, but it is a tale to be told with the rising of another hunter's moon.

The outfitter's work crew struggles to load the author's second massive kudu bull onto a truck for the trip to the skinning shed.

CHAPTER 17

A Dream Realized, Roe Deer

T he photo was of a deer I could not identify, but I loved the way its antlers looked. I backed the chair away from our wood-burning stove and went into the kitchen where my mother was preparing supper. "Mama, what kind of deer is this?" I asked pointing to a photo in a hunting magazine that I had recently received from my uncle, Herbert Aschenbeck. My mother put down the wooden spoon she was using to stir a pot of beef stew and looked intently at the photo, read a bit. "It says it's a roe deer," she said. "They live in England, Germany and Austria."

"Mama one of these days I'm going there to go shoot a roe deer!" I stated looking up at her. She smiled back, probably wondering why a 6-year-old would want to go hunt roe deer. But then perhaps she understood. She too was a hunter and had come from hunting stock, just as had my father. Later that evening she read to me the story in the magazine about a U.S. officer hunting roe deer in Germany, not long after the close of World War II.

I never forgot that story and photo, or the statement I had made to my mother. Always, in the back of my mind, there had been the desire to hunt roe deer. Maybe because quite likely my ancestors had hunted them before they left different parts of Germany and other parts of Europe many years ago to settle in Texas. We still live on some of the land they settled back in the middle 1800s. Today my brother and I still own that property, which was honored a few years ago by the state of Texas as having been involved in agriculture and owned by the same family for over 100 years. Traditions run deep within our direct line of the Weishuhn family, especially when it comes to hunting.

My first encounter with roe deer occurred years ago, when my wife and I traveled to Switzerland for a holiday. While traveling on some of the back roads we spotted roe deer feeding in fields. If I had been interested in roe deer before, now I was hooked. While in Switzerland I purchased a couple of books about roe deer written in German. With my Germanic background, and having spoken German almost exclusively until I started school, I muddled my way through the text, learning all I could about the diminutive deer species. Occasionally I ran into someone who had hunted roe deer in Europe, and when I did, I questioned them unmercifully about what it was like to hunt them, how they were hunted and any other information I could glean.

In time, I started doing television shows and videos with Realtree Camo, and during one of the annual SHOT Shows met Merwyn Manningham Buller, Realtree's sales representative for Europe. Merwyn invited me to come to England to hunt roe deer with him. Unfortunately, the first couple of times my schedule would not allow me to make the trip. Then one day Jim Morey with Swarovski Optiks called to see if I might be interested in going to Austria to see the plant where Swarovski's excellent optics were made. While en route, he said, perhaps we could stop over in England and hunt roe deer with Merwyn.

Thank goodness Jim wasn't there when he mentioned the hunt, because I'm afraid I would have embarrassed myself by giving him a kiss. A prayer had been answered. Finally, well over 40 years after having told my mother I would some day go to Europe to hunt roe deer, I was about to embark on that adventure. The days passed slowly, but I filled them by reading

PREVIOUS PAGES: Hunters search for sign of roe deer in the Dorset countryside in England. Roe deer prefer dense forest with access to farmlands.

As a youngster growing up in rural Texas, the author's mother would often read him stories about roe deer hunting in Europe. Here, he proudly shows off his first roe deer buck, a dream come true.

everything I could about roe deer. I reread articles I'd saved, spending time in the local library, and even getting in touch with biologists I had met from Germany years ago who managed great tracks of land for roe deer. I wanted to know all there was to know about roe deer!

Finally we crawled on board our flight, and several hours later landed at the London airport. After clearing customs, we were picked up by a driver and taken to Merwyn's manor, an ancestral home and estate that belonged to his lovely wife, Lara, and her family. Merwyn leased the surrounding property for hunting. Interestingly, their gracious home had been constructed of stones taken from nearby castles, including nearby Corfe Castle.

Jim and I spent a week as the guests of Merwyn and Lara, hunting roe deer during the daytime and enjoying their hospitality and friendship during the evenings. That week, we enjoyed what I have come to find out was some of the finest roe deer hunting in the world. Merwyn was quite selective in who hunted his lands, and also in what was taken. Only inferior bucks, does and old-age bucks were taken and very few of the latter.

I hunted with Merwyn while Jim hunted with one of Merwyn's assistants. Mostly the hunting was spot and stalk, walking trails along the edges of grassy fields, small woodlots and hedgerows, along the same trails once traveled by medieval knights. Occasionally Merwyn would stop and blow on a shrill-sounding deer call, and quite often either a young buck or a doe responded.

On our first day out, Jim found and ancient 3 by 2 buck, a bit deviant from the normal 3 by 3 racks produced by roe deer. On the scale, the buck field-dressed at 41 pounds. Jim received the antlers, while the meat was properly taken care of and was later sold to help pay for the cost of the lease. We did, however, one evening have excellently prepared roe deer for dinner. Exquisite, absolutely delicious!

Merwyn and I were having a bit more problems getting to the bucks we pursued. Several times the wind switched just as we got close to prime areas that my host knew were frequented by mature bucks. But by the time we got there, all we saw was them disappearing into the tall grass or underbrush.

One afternoon we spotted a grand old buck feeding in a freshly mown hay field. The wind was perfect, but there was insufficient cover to allow for a proper stalk. We were doing great, slowly cutting the distance down to about 300 yards when we happened to rise up, ever so slightly, from our crawling position. There, not 20 yards away stood two sika bucks. They started and turned to run directly toward the roe buck, which disappeared into the thickets at the top of the hill. On another occasion we spotted, at a great distance, a buck feeding near a small creek. We began a slow, steady stalk. Just as we were about to clear some cover that would have given me a shot at the buck, a pickup truck checking on cattle appeared and the big buck disappeared.

A few days after taking his first roe deer, Weishuhn's host, Merwyn Manningham Buller, helped him find this absolutely huge, long-tined roe deer.

INSET:
The antlers of the author's second roe deer were nicely massive at the base.

We got close to that buck twice and each time he managed to give us the slip. According to Merwyn, he had watched the buck grow into a massively antlered deer. If anything, he might be a bit past prime, making for a most interesting trophy. I did get one glimpse of him, and having looked at several roe deer racks, which were considered quite excellent, I knew the buck we had stalked would have rated high in the European scoring system. So went our stalks day after day. It was beginning to look as if I might have to return to England for another roe deer engagement. Then finally things changed.

One morning as we drove to another area to hunt, I spotted a buck as we passed a field full of tall grass. I mentioned the buck to Merwyn, who stopped and glassed the buck that was feeding in the broad, relatively open field. "Definitely mature! but lacking in tine length. One we should try to remove," he said in proper British English. Those words were music and magic to my ears. We parked the car some distance away and began our stalk. Taking advantage of a line of oak trees, we were able to cut the distance to about 200 yards. From there I belly crawled to another oak and got about 25 yards closer. The tree roots provided a perfect rest. When the beautifully stocked .25-06 rifle barked, the deer fell quickly to the ground.

No sooner than I had shot him, I wanted to go see my roe deer. "Stay down!" came the command from Merwyn. "Huge buck behind us, one I've wanted taken for the past two years. Absolute monster!" I obeyed and turned careful-

Dorset's 13th-century Corfe Castle, now in ruins, stands in fabulous roe deer country. Other species in the area include the imported Japanese sika deer and England's last population of red squirrels.

INSET:
Jim Morey with the bronze medal roe deer that he took in the shadow of the walls of Corfe Castle

ly to look for the big deer. I spotted him immediately. His antlers were tall, with long brow and secondary points, and they were massive from the base to the end.

We watched as the buck disappeared into some tall grass near the end of the pasture and began a careful and circuitous stalk. I wish I could tell you we found and took that buck, but we didn't. We never saw him again. Where he went, we'll never know. After the failed stalk we came back to my first roe deer. I could not have been more pleased if I had just taken a world record. Finally, I had taken a roe deer and life was good!

On the following day, Merwyn mentioned that he would let me take a second buck if we could find one of the truly old and big deer. Based on our past luck I doubted that would happen, but I knew it would be fun to try! We decided to hunt a buck that Merwyn had watched for the past three years. He'd only tried for the buck once and it had given him the slip. That afternoon the wind was "right."

We entered the pasture and trailed along the

edge of a small brook. A few minutes later we spotted a great roe deer. Instead of the normal 3 by 3 rack, it was a 4 by 5, with one extra point on one side and two on the other. We stalked to within about 75 yards. "He's on the wrong side of the brook," said Merwyn. "My property line is the little creek. If he were on this side we'd take him."

It was as if the buck read the Englishman's mind, for he immediately turned and walked over the small hill on the safe side. We bid him adieu and headed deeper into the property. About 10 minutes later, Merwyn stopped abruptly and stared through his field glasses at a distant buck. "It's him, the one we want . . . Let's go!" With that we took off at a run toward the feeding buck.

Reaching a point about 75 yards distant from the buck, we stopped under a tree, which made a convenient rifle rest. "Shoot him," instructed Merwyn. I did. At the shot, the buck jumped and ran about 25 yards before going down. My well-composed English friend let out a whoop, jumped the small brook that separated us and ran toward the downed buck. I followed suit as fast as I could.

As we neared the buck's side, Merwyn turned, grabbed me and gave me a hug. "You've done it. You've got him. He's huge, absolutely huge, could likely be one of the best bucks taken this year in England." That said a lot because I knew England produced some of the best roe deer in all of Europe.

On the following day we did some photography and then headed out to find Jim a second buck, hunting nearly in the shadow of Corfe Castle. From a high ridge overlooking the castle we spotted a sizable roe buck. Immediately Jim and Merwyn planned a long stalk. It took some doing, but finally they got in position for Jim to take a shot. Several minutes later I helped him photograph his silver medal buck with the Castle Corfe in the background.

If I lived closer to where roe deer lived, they would quickly become my favorite big game animal, just as they are a favorite of most of the European hunters. In taking my two English roe deer, I had realized a dream begun many years earlier. That dream has now been amended. I want to hunt roe deer again, not only in England but in other parts of Europe as well. It's good to know the hunter's moon rises from the east, and its rising will someday beckon me for a return engagement. I can hardly wait!

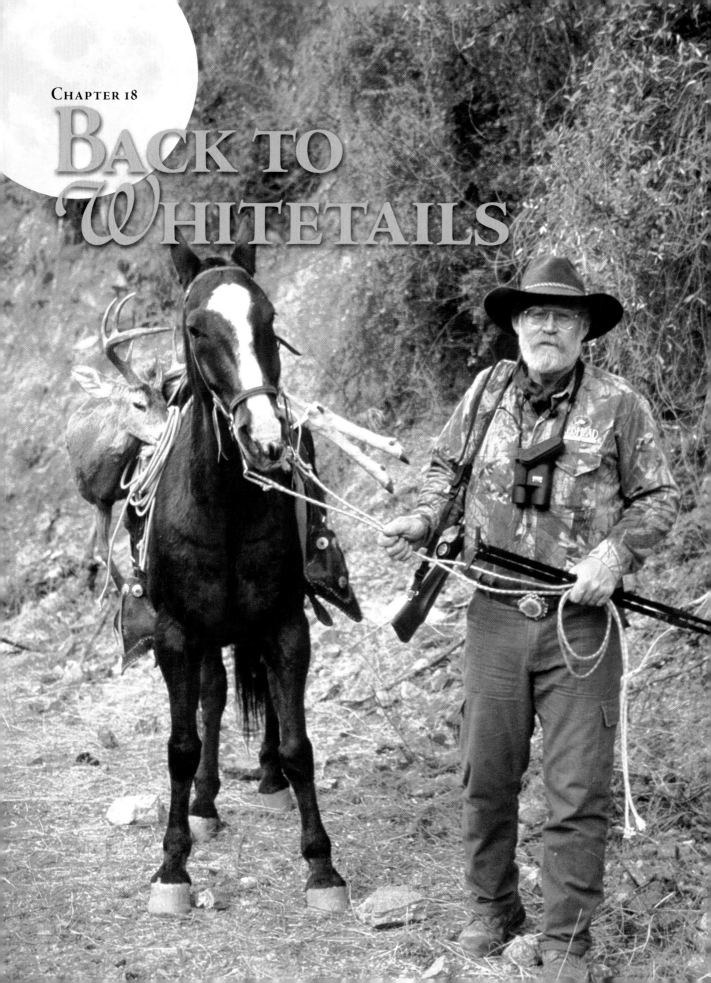

CHAPTER 18

BACK TO WHITETAILS

Awriter once said, "You can't go home again." He was wrong! For me, at least, whitetail hunting is like going home regardless of where their home is. To put it another way, I feel at home in the whitetail woods, farmland, brush country or semi-open prairie. Of all the game I've hunted thus far, my favorite remains the grand whitetail deer.

The whitetail is highly adaptable and makes his home in the wild or in urban areas. A few years ago I saw one of the biggest bucks I've ever seen in Texas, practically in downtown Houston. I've also seen big-antlered bucks on the edges of many Midwestern towns, where they feed at night on fertilized roses and other "introduced browse." I've also seen whitetails live on open prairies that, I had assumed, were considerably better pronghorn antelope habitat than whitetail country. I've also seen a few living just below timberline in the Rocky Mountains and in the provincial forests of Canada, just below the tundra. Areas of Mexico, which most whitetail hunters would view as not being abundant enough to support jackrabbits and rattlesnakes, often hold great bucks.

Whitetail populations have flourished during the past century, reaching greater highs than before Europeans came to this continent. Those of us who hunted the last third of the 20th century and the first years of the 21st century have experienced the greatest white-tailed deer hunting this world has ever known. I'd like to think it will continue that way for many years, and likely it will. However, changes will have to be made in some areas regarding deer densities. Anytime there is overpopulation, regardless of the species, nature has a

OPPOSITE:
Larry Weishuhn packs a Coues buck out of the mountains in New Mexico. The secretive and cunning Coues whitetails live in remote and rugged habitat which makes for a truly challenging hunt.

The author finds that hunting mature bucks with a handgun is a challenging endeavor. The Thompson/Center Encore is his favorite hunting weapon.

way of correcting the situation, and it normally does so in a much harsher and crueler manner than if it is accomplished by man.

As a wildlife biologist who promoted quality deer herd and habitat management for years, it's been interesting to see the changes that have occurred during the past years. Some of those changes have been for the good of the species, but some have also been for the good of a certain portion of the human population's ego and pocket books. When I started hunting, to gain access to privately owned hunting ground, you simply asked permission, or you helped the farmer or rancher with his chores. Now some people pay more money to take a single whitetail than the amount I paid for our first home! That is not all bad. It is because of interest in bigger antlers and bodies in white-tailed deer that we have learned much about the species.

We hunt whitetails for a variety of reasons, ranging from population control to providing food for our families. Others honor the bucks we take by having them mounted as trophies for our walls to help us recall each and every minute detail of the hunt. Some enjoy spending quality time with friends and family and others hunt for the pure joy of pursuing whitetails and having fun. In my opinion, all these are valid reasons to hunt "America's deer."

I also believe it is man's innate nature to hunt. Regrettably, while those of us who enjoy hunting pursue game, those who oppose antihunting expend their energies trying to prevent us from doing so. Unfortunately, those who don't hunt are often responsible for the demise of species and habitat. Species and populations bounce back relatively quickly, but habitat, once it is altered, takes many years to recover. Sometimes it requires the span of many human lifetimes to do so, if indeed it ever does.

For Larry Weishuhn the hunt for big, mature whitetails, no matter where they live, is challenging. The experience of hunting mature bucks is completely different than the pursuit of "ordinary deer."

Whitetails are important to me. And I dearly love to hunt them! Mostly I enjoy hunting mature whitetails, which have attained the age of four years old or older. Such bucks have experienced life, have done their bit for procreation, and have learned the ways of the hunter. They are challenging to say the least. In so saying, I realize whitetailed deer are somewhat like people. All of us know some extremely intelligent people that are also "street-wise," and we also likely know a few that lack a bit in terms of survival skills.

In most instances, by the time a buck reaches four years of age he has learned survival skills that will challenge even the best of hunters. These are the bucks that will lie in a patch of grass and let hunters walk right by them. These are also the bucks that have a way of inhabiting places where hunters do not normally go. If indeed they are taken, they are generally taken by a novice who didn't "know" that you don't hunt broad open fields, or just beyond someone's backyard, or in a patch of brush that no one else hunts because there has never been a deer seen there. Sometimes I think we "experienced deer hunters" think we know more than we actually do. Playing dumb, however, does not often lead to taking a good, mature deer.

Several years ago I worked with the management programs on several ranches. Our approach to quality management was rather simple. Give the bucks a chance to mature in the presence of quality forage and nutrition. That meant, in some instances, reducing the overall population while at the same time bringing up not only the quantity but also the quality of the food available to them on a daily (and not seasonal) basis.

After several of these programs had been in operation for four or more years, I often had property owners and hunters come to me and question the quality of the deer on their property. "We don't think we've seen a huge increase in quality, at least not what we expected." "Our younger bucks look better but we can't seem to find many of our older bucks. What gives?"

Generally at that point, I would call the local game warden and make arrangements for him to accompany us on a nighttime spotlight foray through the property. After dark, by using a light, I could show the landowner and his hunters many big, mature bucks, bucks that were hardly ever seen during daylight hours. If some of these bigger bucks moved at all during the day, it was generally during the middle of the day when hunters were back at camp either eating or napping.

Are such nocturnal bucks killable? Sometimes and sometimes not! Occasionally one of the truly nocturnal bucks will make a daytime mistake. The key to taking him is being in the woods when he does! Want to shoot a mature buck? Hunt where they exist, and then go hunting and hunt all day long!

I recall one particular mature 6-pointer, which was an extremely active breeder based on the many other 6-point bucks we saw in the immediate area where he lived. I wanted badly to remove the old buck, desiring the breeding to be done by

White-tailed deer remain the most popular big game animal in North America.

multitined bucks. I tried every legal way I could to take the deer, but all was for naught! I could find him at night with a light, but that was the only time. Over the course of a couple of years, I tried every legal means to remove this particular buck. All failed. In doing so, however, I learned much about the deer. And, he likely learned just as much about me!

One day during the middle of the hunting season, while walking through an extremely dense thicket I found three of the 6-pointer's cast antlers. The thicket was only about 25 yards long and rather narrow. Inside the thicket were also several fresh beds. The following morning, a cold north blustery wind was blowing. I got up at 3:00 a.m., dressed and headed to the thicket. I sat down in the southern third of it, fully camouflaged from head to toe. First light would not occur until about 7:00 that morning. I settled in for a long, cold wait.

At about 6:15, I heard a deer walk into the thicket and bed down only about six or eight steps to the north of me. I dared not move. Thankfully the hard wind blowing through the thicket covered the sounds of my breathing. About 30 minutes later, when a particularly hard gust of wind blew, I raised my rifle, pointed it in the direction of where I thought the deer was bedded, rested it on a snag and waited.

Ever so slowly the light conditions improved. Little by little I could discern the outline of a bedded deer facing away from me. As the gray light brightened I could see it was a buck with 6 points. Knowing it was now well beyond legal shooting light, I waited for another strong gust of wind to blow through the thicket and quietly thumbed back the hammer. When I pulled the trigger on the old Winchester Model 94, the deer simply dropped his head. My two-year quest was over! Hunting skill? No not really, simply getting lucky and taking advantage of the situation. I had walked through the thicket initially because it was one of the few small thickets I had never walked through before. Doing so lead me to the animal I truly hoped to take. The old 6-pointer was truly a trophy in every way. But then I consider every animal I've ever taken a "trophy."

During the years, I have spent considerable time in a helicopter doing game survey as part of management programs and have seen lots of big bucks. I used to keep a record of the total number of bucks I saw, but quit after the number exceeded 500,000. Interestingly, of the truly big bucks, only a very small percentage were ever taken by hunters — less than one-tenth of one percent.

Back then I often hunted individual bucks that I had spotted from the air. I hunted them hard, starting early in the season and then hunted them throughout the season but I never did see them while hunting. Had I not known better, I would have sworn they were killed by fellow hunters, poached, or became a meal for coyotes or a mountain lion. But, the following fall there they would be, back in the same areas where we had previously seen them.

I have hunted whitetails for about 50 years now, and I'm as excited about hunting them today as I was when I first started. Over the years I have learned a lot, but there is still much more to learn. Will I hunt other big game species? Most definitely there are many places and animals I yearn to hunt, and many big game fields I hope to return to. But, one thing for certain, I'll always look forward to coming home and hunting whitetails!

The European red deer has been transplanted to nearly every continent. As with whitetail bucks every red stag is an individual.

INDEX